MUSLIMS IN THE WEST

The Message and Mission

D1596269

SYED ABUL HASAN ALI NADWI

Edited by
Khurram Murad

The Islamic Foundation

ISBN 0 86037 130 1 (Paperback)
ISBN 0 86037 131 X (Hardback)

Published by
The Islamic Foundation
223 London Road
Leicester LE2 1ZE, United Kingdom

Quran House
P.O. Box 30611, Nairobi, Kenya

PMB 3196, Kano, Nigeria

British Library Cataloguing in Publication Data
  Nadvi, Abulhasan Ali
    Muslims in the west
    1. Muslims
    I. Title   II. Murad, Khurram
    305.6'2971'01812   D810.M5

ISBN 0-86037-131-X
ISBN 0-86037-130-1 Pbk

Printed by
Dotesios (Printers) Limited
Bradford-on-Avon, Wiltshire.

Contents

Editor's Preface

Syed Abul Hasan Ali Nadwi's outstanding contributions to the cause of Islam in our age are well-known. He is an eminent scholar, a powerful, eloquent writer and orator, both in Urdu and Arabic. No complete bibliography of his numerous works (many of which have appeared in English translation) has yet been prepared: his speeches and writing have charm, force, penetration; more than that, they radiate a passionate sincerity that goes straight to the heart.

Among various important themes he has addressed are the relationship between Islam and the West, the plight of the West, and the situation and role of Muslims living in the West. The English translation of a collection of his three speeches, delivered in Britain in 1963, 1964 and 1969, together with three articles, was published under the title, *Speaking Plainly to the West* (Lucknow, 1973). In the summer of 1977, he visited the United States and Canada at the invitation of the Muslim Students' Association, mainly to attend their Annual Convention. During that visit, he delivered a number of speeches at various centres in many important cities in the U.S. and Canada. An English translation of those speeches appeared under the title *From the Depth of the Heart in America* (Lucknow, 1978), translated from Urdu by Mohammad Asif Kidwai. Both books offer valuable insights into the predicament of Western civilisation, its strengths and weaknesses, and discuss at some length the role and responsibilities of Muslims living in the West.

The present book, *Muslims in the West: the Message and Mission* is a result of amalgamating and extensively editing both the above works. The language has been improved with the invaluable help of Dr. Z. J. Qureshi, who deserves our profound thanks for his important contribution and hard labours. Further, I have totally rearranged the papers to

5

bring out better their continuity and coherence. One lecture given to students receiving modern education has been omitted. A fresh article, 'Islam: The Most Suitable Religion for Mankind', has been added from Islamic Council of Europe's *The Challenge of Islam* (ed. Altaf Gauhar, London, 1978) with the permission of Mr. Salem Azzam, its Secretary General, to whom our thanks are due.

Such a series of lectures, delivered before similar audiences, at the same time, in different places, inevitably repeats some material. But the themes of the book are so absorbing, the message so urgent and so feelingly expressed that the repetitions are nowhere irksome to the reader. Moreover, because the style of oratory has a value and charm of its own, different from that of the written word, every effort has been made to preserve it.

The present book, after rearranging the earlier material, is divided into two parts: Part One — The West: Its Predicament and the Message of Islam — consists of seven chapters. They address mainly the West, analysing its history, characteristics, achievements and shortcomings; and inviting it to Islam as the only suitable and viable way of life for mankind, while explaining the historical reasons for the West's attitude towards Islam. Part Two — Muslims: The Mission and the Community — consists of nine chapters which address mainly Muslims living in the West, outlining and emphasising their mission and role in the West as ambassadors of Islam, examining their situation, cautioning them against the dangers they face while living in an un-Islamic environment and defining the ways and means through which they can safeguard their faith and identity.

The major themes emerge loud and clear. Nadwi sees no reason why the West and the East should always remain at loggerheads. Both have their strengths and weaknesses. He acknowledges ungrudgingly the advances in science and technology, and the material progress, made by the West, and asks Muslims to learn what the West has to offer them. Yet the East possesses certain treasures which the West does not: treasures of the Divine guidance which illumined man's inner recesses, nurtured his spiritual resources, quickened his heart, sharpened his intellect and lifted him to sublime heights of nobility. Unfortunately the West has been unable to drink from the founts of life that spring in the East. The reasons are many: Christianity — its dogmas, its opposition to advances in human knowledge leading to the West's rejection of all religion, and the failures of Muslims themselves — their inability to live up to Islam and bring its message to the West.

The only escape Nadwi sees for the West, that may rescue it from the consequences of its own follies, at the same time reconciling East and West and so unifying mankind, is to embrace the Divine guidance brought by the Prophets of God. His analysis of the West, though passionate and, at times, harsh, is convincing. The West's entire concern is with man's outer world; it is totally indifferent to the world that lies inside him. Having refused to submit to One God, it has become a slave to its own progress and technology. Devoid of faith, material progress, though at its pinnacle, is hollow. Technology has placed vast powers in the hands of Western man, which enable him, for the first time, to annihilate himself; yet it has not equipped him to handle these powers in the interest of mankind. The West's attitudes are characterised by a sense of arrogant superiority towards all those living beyond its frontiers. This in itself has become a major impediment in its way to coming to Islam, apart from all the historical reasons.

As for Muslims, Nadwi insists that their presence in the West can have only one justification: to communicate the message of Islam to their fellow human beings here, both by words and example. Even though they might have come for reasons other than Islamic, to get money or education or both, this duty is foremost. A Muslim cannot exist as a Muslim unless he fulfils the mission entrusted to him by Allah and His Prophet. It is, according to Nadwi, an unfortunate accident of history that the West could neither perceive the blessings of Islam nor receive them. That the great human potential of the West could not bloom fully for the better service of mankind is a consequence of its rejection of the Divine guidance, the Divine light was not allowed to penetrate the darkness. The blame, Nadwi tells Muslims in unmistakable terms, rests also upon their shoulders. Now is the opportunity for them to make amends for past failures.

He also makes an incisive analysis of the situation prevailing in Muslim countries as a result of the impact of Western colonialism and 'civilisation'. An unbridgeable gulf separates the Westernised rulers of these countries and the Muslim masses. Though political freedom has been gained, at least on the surface, cultural serfdom has deepened. Young Muslim students who must go back to their countries will there face the acute crisis which is resulting in huge wastage of Muslim energies and talents. The theme is greatly relevant for there is little doubt that Muslim students form a significant part of the Muslim community in the West, and they are sure to occupy positions of power and prestige when they return to their countries of origin. Nadwi brings home to them the weaknesses of the culture in which they are living as well as of that to which they will go back.

Various chapters take up, coherently and logically, the concerns outlined above. Chapter one starts by looking into the gulf that separates the Muslim East and the Christian West. It explores the impact of the Crusades, colonialism and Orientalism in creating and perpetuating a relationship of suspicion, fear and hostility between the two cultures and stresses that the message of the Prophets of God, which elevates man to the status of His vicegerency and proclaims the unity of mankind, can be the only basis for reconciliation between them.

Chapter two attempts to find the reasons which inhibit the West from accepting the message of the Prophets of God. Tracing the history of Greece and Rome and that of the sixth century world followed by the subsequent presence of Muslims in Spain, it identifies pride and arrogance as the main obstacle preventing the West from seeing the truth of the Prophetic message.

Chapter three turns to Germany. Recognising its radical contributions to the thought and philosophy of the West, its qualities of innovation and industry, and its unsuccessful bids for world leadership, Nadwi laments that Germany too should have been unable to break the mould and chart a new course for herself and for Western civilisation. The world needs Islam; any nation may come forward and take the lead.

Why not Germany?

America, the paradise of material progress, is the subject of Chapter four. Here the malady is not difficult to trace: despite the abundance of material goods it refuses to recognise the sovereignty of One God, whose writ runs supreme in the universe.

Chapter five shows how man, in refusing to be a slave to the One God becomes a slave to his own creations, his technology, his machines. This spiritual poverty is depicted specifically in the American context.

The tragic consequences of the fact that Islam did not reach America and the West are dealt with in Chapter six, where all Muslims living in America are exhorted to take up, now, the duty of bringing this message to Americans.

Chapter seven, explaining that Islam is the only suitable way of life for mankind, serves to link Part One and Part Two.

That Muslims should live as emissaries of Islam and, whatever the odds, deliver its message to America is the theme of Chapter eight.

Chapter nine argues that there is no cause for Muslims to despair in this task, provided they have faith and trust in God. With that faith and trust, Muslims coming out of Arabia in the early years of Islam were able to overcome the vast empires of Rome and Persia.

Chapters ten and eleven, then turn to some specific issues that immigrants must face up to as an ideological community. They stress in particular the importance of an Islamic environment, based on brotherhood, for the preservation and strengthening of faith and Islamic identity, without which Muslims can neither live as Muslims nor discharge their mission. But only faith and love for Allah and His Messenger can be the enduring and stable foundation for a truly Islamic brotherhood, emphasises Chapter twelve.

Chapter thirteen spells out some specific, valuable advice for Muslim immigrants in the West so that they may live as Muslims and raise their children as Muslims. Chapter fourteen, addressed to Muslim women, emphasises the strength of the relationship of interdependence and love between man and woman, established in the name of Allah,

9

and makes it clear that, as Muslims, they both have the same responsibilities. Chapters fifteen and sixteen are addressed to young Muslims living in the West whether for study or work. After describing the situation in the West and the Muslim countries, it tells them to resist being swamped by the alien culture within which they live, to boldly present the message of Islam, and to prepare themselves for the responsibilities that await their return home.

I have no illusion that I can add anything of value to Nadwi's arguments. Yet I allow myself the liberty of the following brief note in the hope that, in the context of Muslim presence in the West, it may contribute something to the understanding of the long-standing relationship between Islam and the West and, therefore, help in the task of *da'wah* which Nadwi has so emphatically and persistently demanded of Muslims.

'History and geography alike dictated that Islam and the West should come into close contact', writes Dr. I. H. Qureshi, a noted Pakistani scholar of Islam. This contact dates from the very advent of Islam. Yet, despite continuing contact, unbridgeable distances exist between the two. Western perceptions of Islam have been shaped to suit the West's political and economic interests. While it may be true that Muslims made very little attempt to study Christianity from its original sources — perhaps they never considered Christianity to be a problem for them — it cannot be claimed that, during recent times, Muslims have been backward in their study of Western civilisation and thought. Moreover, while the West may certainly claim to have done more to study Islam, it has as certainly never been able to take an objective view in its studies. The reasons that brought Islam and the West into conflict have been hinted at by Nadwi. Anyone interested in finding out more from unbiased sources will profit by reading Norman Daniel's *Islam and the West: The Making of an Image* (Edinburgh, 1980); *The Arabs and Medieval Europe* (Longman, London, 1979); *Islam, Europe and Empire* (Edinburgh, 1966); and R. W. Southern's *Western View of Islam in the Middle Ages* (Harvard University Press, Cambridge, 1961).

Muslims have been in Europe for long periods in history.

They ruled over Spain for more than 700 years (711 – 1492) but were finally defeated and totally eliminated; not a single Muslim survived, no trace was allowed to remain. They were in Sicily for 260 years (831 – 1091) yet their fate was no different from that in Spain. The Ottoman Turks were in Eastern Europe — they camped on the banks of the River Danube and knocked at the doors of Vienna — but they too shrank back. It is only now that many millions of Muslims have made Europe their home and are living as members of a secular pluralist society. After Christianity, Islam is the second largest faith in many European countries. Exact figures are hard to come by, but rough estimates show that some two million Muslims live in each of Britain, France and Germany. Islam is gradually being given official recognition in countries where such recognition is legally possible, as in Austria and Belgium. Muslims live as next door neighbours to non-Muslims; they contribute as workers and supervisors in their factories and offices; they teach and study in their institutions of learning — they form a part of the nation's life. Also, for the first time, indigenous Muslim communities, though small in number, dot the landscape of Europe.

All this signals a historic situation — both with a unique potential and an enormous danger. Muslims may either become assimilated in the surrounding culture and, over generations, lose their identity. Or, they may decide to live as Muslims, as emissaries of Islam, and assert and communicate their faith and way of life. This may have two results: either they will, at least, continue to survive and live as a distinct group and contribute some of their rich faith and culture to the West. Or, they will win over the West to Islam by succeeding in radically changing the prevalent culture and shaping it in the mould of Divine guidance.

Nadwi calls upon them to adopt a twofold strategy: on the one hand, they should concentrate on safeguarding their faith, protect their rising generations, maintain their links with their countries of origin, and eschew alien cultural manners and influences. On the other hand, they should strive to fulfil their mission and make every effort to bring the message of Islam to the men and women alongside whom they live and work.

11

I hope and trust that Muslims in the West will respond positively to Nadwi's passionate call which bids them rouse their hearts and minds. They will realise the responsibilities that they owe to themselves, to the *Ummah,* to the society they live in and, finally, to God. They will realise that they possess a rich inheritance, that of Divine guidance, and they have a duty to convey it to the West. It would be tragic if they, owning the blessing of Islam, should become beggars and succumb to Western modes of thought and living. Let them hear Rūmī:

> There is an illimitable fountain of milk within thee: Why art thou seeking milk from the pail?
> O lake, thou hast a channel to the Sea; be ashamed to seek water from the pool;
> . . .
>
> There is a basket full of loaves on the crown of thy head, and thou art begging a crust of bread from door to door.
>
> Attend to thine own head, abandon giddy headedness; go knock at the door of thy heart: why art thou (knocking) at every door?
>
> Whilst thou art up to the knee in the river water, thou art heedless of thy self and art seeking water from this one and that one.
> Water in front; and behind too, an unfailing supply of water; (but) before thine eyes is *a barrier* and *behind them a barrier.*
>
> (*The Mathnawī,* Vol.VI, ed. and tr. R. A. Nicholson, p.66.)

But, at the same time, they must be open minded and generously recognise any merits or contributions that the West has made towards the advancement of human knowledge and civilisation. They should not hesitate to exchange wisely and diligently within their own cultural framework. At no time in history has there been a total bar on cultural exchange, nor should one be attempted now. If Muslims try to impose one, the influences will still somehow creep in. A wiser and better policy is to keep the initiative and, after critical evaluation, adopt what can be adopted within the framework of Islam.

I thank Syed Abul Hasan Ali Nadwi whose affection and generosity have made the publication of this book possible. The editing, while improving the book in some respects, may also have introduced certain elements of error for which the blame is entirely ours. May Allah reward him here and in the Hereafter for his immense services for the cause of Islam. I hope the Islamic Foundation will be able to publish more of his works in future.

May Allah in His infinite mercy accept our humble efforts and forgive our mistakes and sins.

The Islamic Foundation,   **Khurram Murad**
Leicester   Director General
Jumāda al-Ūlā 1403
March 1983

Introduction*

The fundamental problem of modern Islam is how to get Muslim society to forge ahead with renewed vigour, power and drive as a Divinely-guided society should and must. This question has exercised the minds of Muslims ever since the opening decades of the nineteenth century when they found themselves enfeebled by decadence within and confronted by the growing might of the West striding forth in their lands in explosive restlessness. Their immediate reaction, and quite natural too, was that of a zealot who opposes the political and military expansion of his adversary with all his might and at all costs. The leaders of the Islamic East saw the West as something primarily to be rejected; they protested against its external encroachment as well as its corrupting influence: their condemnation of everything Western was deep yet narrow. They summoned the Muslim society back to its original purity and order; but having lost the capacity to order its life effectively, to refashion it morally, intellectually and materially, the result achieved by them was not unexpected. Not only did the East, including Muslim countries, pass into the political domination of the West, one after another, but it lost its self-confidence too with the failure of its efforts. On the other hand, the West launching forth with the greatest upsurge and expansive energy it had summoned up in its history, took the offensive from diverse directions — it was an unrelenting attack on a politically decadent and intellectually stagnant East from the directions of philosophy as well as economics, literature as well as science, politics as well as culture.

---

*This was the Introduction to *Speaking Plainly to the West,* Lucknow, 1973, a collection of lectures and essays by Abul Hasan Ali Nadwi, which are all now included in the present book.

The consolidation of political as well as intellectual superiority of the West produced another group of persons who, taking its superiority for granted, directed their protest solely against internal deterioration of the community. They advocated complete acceptance of the Western mode of life and way of thinking as the only way to achieve political freedom; they wanted to carry the whole community as passive adherents along the tide of Western liberalism that flowed around. They desired to harmonise the East with the West, but the harmonising sought by them was more passive and permissive than active and creative. They tried to redefine the content or the methods of faith in the light of Western liberalism and some were even bold enough to declare that Islam would perish unless it came to terms with the modern world. The *Sharī'ah* was considered by them as outmoded and inferior to the Western legal system; they stigmatised the transcendental values of life as backward, medieval and reactionary. But their undue emphasis on worldly outlook succeeded only in producing apologetics for the external intrusion and menace, and a class struggle and schism in the community for decadence within.

However, both these groups — those protesting against external encroachment and those condemning internal deterioration — failed to correctly estimate the real dimensions of the problem. None of them could adequately assess the ambitions, roots and causes of the exuberant Europe nor could anyone generate a new synthesis of the East and West that might incite their people into constructing new dreams and adventures. If one failed to understand the secret springs of power wielded by the West, the other was carried away by its blind acceptance of everything Western and modern. If one vehemently rejected the West, the other passively accepted it as an inevitable must; but, none tried to meet it on terms of equality and mutual understanding.

In the lectures and essays included in this volume, the author points to a third course. He reviews the situation in comprehensive terms in its true perspective and advocates that the vitality and skill of the West should be appropriated rather than accepted. He wants the East to be enlightened rather than intoxicated by the West. At the same time, he urges the Muslim East to maintain its distinctive individuality, its faith, its moral integrity and fervidness of heart and spirit; since, on its ability to do so depends its capacity to play a useful role for itself, for the West and for humanity at large. He focuses attention on the fact, vividly clear yet overlooked by the critics as well as eulogisers of Western civilisation, that the modern West is moved by the philosophic vision of ancient Greece which demands a complete separation of all institutions, customs, ideas, arts and sciences from religion, rejects everything beyond the visible and tangible and makes man a measure of all things. He brings out how these bases of Western thought and culture are antagonistic and incompatible with the values and ideals cherished by Islam as well as destructive to the West itself. Nevertheless, his thought-provoking criticism of Western intellectualism — its materialistic view of life, its failure in social and moral spheres and the resultant chaos threatening the entire world with moral and social disintegration — is neither destructive nor produced by an emotion of revengeful hatred of the West.

He underlines, on the one hand, the inner contradiction of the modern material progress — the contradiction of its astounding achievements in the physical field and failure on social, moral and spiritual fronts and, on the other, the capacity of the East to help the West out of its present predicament. He wants the Muslim East to understand the real cause of material prosperity and worldly success of the West, accept only what is worthwhile, and, in return, help the West in overcoming its own follies and shortcomings, aberrations and excesses for their mutual benefit. He asks the East to guard and conserve its own latent energies of faith and righteousness, intellectual integrity and moral strength, and build a new bridge across which humanity may walk to mutual understanding, progress and prosperity, material advancement as well as spiritual enrichment to create a brave new world — a world that would be worth living in for all, for the white and the black, for the great and the small, for the powerful and the weak.

Mohiuddin Ahmad

17

Foreword*

In the Name of Allah, the Beneficent, the Merciful

This is a collection of my speeches given in the United States and Canada which I visited in the summer of 1977. I went there at the invitation of the Muslim Students' Association, mainly to attend its Annual Conference at Bloomington in Indiana. After the Conference, a tour was arranged by the Association which took me to almost all the important cities and educational, cultural and industrial centres of North America where a considerable number of Muslims drawn from India, Pakistan and the Arab countries live for various reasons. The original itinerary included New York City, Jersey City, Philadelphia, Baltimore, Boston, Chicago, Detroit, Salt Lake City, San Francisco, San Jose and Los Angeles in the States, and Montreal and Toronto in Canada, to which Washington was added later.

In all, I addressed twenty gatherings, half of them in Arabic and half in Urdu. I had an opportunity to speak at five leading American universities — the Columbia University at New York, the Harvard University at Cambridge, the Detroit University at Ann Arbor, the South Californian University at Los Angeles and the Utah University at Salt Lake City — and was, also, asked to give the Friday sermon in the Prayer Hall at the United Nations Headquarters and in the Jāmiʻ Masjids of Toronto and Detroit. Muslims who are studying in America or have taken up residence there took a keen interest in the meetings and came from near and far to attend them.

---

*This was the Foreword by the author as included in *From the Depth of the Heart in America,* Lucknow, 1978, a collection of lectures delivered by him in America, which are all now included in the present book.

In the haste of moving from place to place it was not possible to collect the tapes of all the speeches. The transcriptions contained in this volume were prepared, largely, by Syed Mushtaq Ahmad Bhopali of Darul Ulum Nadwatul Ulama, Lucknow, from the tapes I was able to bring with me. Before I could revise the written copies of the speeches, most of them were published in *Ta'mīr-i-Millat,* the fortnightly organ of Nadwatul Ulama, for which I am thankful to its Editor, Ibrahim Jalis Nadwi. Had the printed versions of the speeches not been made available to me, it would have taken much more time and labour to prepare the present volume. The speeches in Arabic, except for the translations of two of them, have not been included in this collection. These will be published separately from Beirut or Cairo.

It is hoped that this booklet will be read with interest, both in India and abroad, and that friends residing in America who had listened to the speeches directly as well as those who could not or did not do so will find something in them deserving of serious thought.

For fellow countrymen it is a 'gift' of the trip to America and for the friends and well-wishers in America, a 'requital' of the kindness and affection shown by them.

If there is any justification for the publication of these speeches it is the attempt at plain-speaking that has been made in them. My constant endeavour has been to speak straight from the heart, without mincing words, and to offer some sincere suggestions to the Muslim brothers and sisters who have settled in the West, particularly in America. As for the Western civilisation, it has been viewed from a height which Islam confers upon its followers and from which both the Old and the New Worlds seem narrow and empty, and their glitter false and unreal. The credit for this particular way of looking at things does not belong to me but to the Guidance and Message which imparts a new vision to man and causes the scales to fall from his eyes.

I take the opportunity to express my sincere gratitude to all the friends who helped to make the journey such a rewarding experience and looked after my needs and comfort with unceasing care and affection. They make a long list, but mention must be made of the names of Syed Naziruddin Ali Hyderabadi, the Vice-President and Programme-Incharge, Mr. Anis Ahmad, the Director of Education, Publicity and Information, Dr. Mahmud Rushdan, the General Secretary, and Dr. Yaqub Mirza, the President of the Muslim Students' Association who spared no pains to make my stay as useful and comfortable as possible.

May Allah requite them bounteously and bestow His good pleasure upon them.

Daira-i-Shah Ilmullah   **Abul Hasan Ali Nadwi**
Rae Bareli
December 20, 1977

21

PART I

THE WEST
Its Predicament and the Message of Islam

Chapter One

East and West

The Muslim East and the Christian West, though members of the same human family, have been living in confrontation and conflict for centuries. The gulf that separates them seems to be unbridgeable; reconciliation and harmony appear to be impossible. At a time when human society stands divided as never before this state of relationship between its two most important components is fraught with grave dangers for the future of mankind. Nadwi sees no reason why this situation should continue.

He identifies some of the factors which are responsible for creating this state of affairs, and for preserving it: ignorance and superficial knowledge, distorted images, conflict of interests which have bred distrust and hostility. The shadows cast by the Crusades looked more real as colonialism advanced to grab one Muslim country after another in the nineteenth century. Colonialists came not only as rulers and exploiters, but as masters and civilisers. They subverted culture and implanted their own ideologies, like nationalism. Even Orientalism, a scholarly discipline, despite its achievements, failed to inform the West of the truth about Islam and Muslims, of what the East could offer to the West.

Nadwi, then, leads on to the Prophets appearing in the East, who concentrated upon 'man' rather than his external world. They opened up his huge potential of energy. They invented neither tools nor machinery, but a new man. Their message and methodology stand in sharp contrast to the recent Western approach. The disastrous consequences of the Western preoccupation with the physical nature as against the spiritual are obvious. In faith, residing in the heart, lies the key to man's ultimate success, a faith which the West does not possess. The gulf between East and West is the gulf between faith and science.

Only the faith as offered by the Prophets, Nadwi argues, even today, can bring the East and the West together. [Ed.]

1

'East is East and West is West', Kipling wrote; and added, to clinch the matter, 'And ne'er the twain shall meet'. It often happens that a poet finds fitting words to express a thought that has come to be widely accepted in a society and has played an important role in the formation of its beliefs and feelings. And then the thought becomes proverbial; it is held more firmly, is the more easily remembered.

Kipling in that famous couplet epitomised the idea so long accepted, by East and West alike, that there must be this perpetual division of the human family. Certainly, I venture to say, I have not come across any literary expression that has done more harm to the hope for the unity of mankind. No matter how seemingly innocent and natural Kipling's words may be, no matter how accurately they may describe an historical situation, expressions of this kind have contributed a great deal towards the preservation of East and West as hostile and irreconcilable. If ever, they seem to meet only to battle, with arms or words.

For centuries East and West have remained at a distance, either in complete ignorance or possessing only extremely superficial knowledge of each other. Each has seen in the other rather its weakness and ugliness than its strength and beauty. Their mutual behaviour has hitherto been determined in an atmosphere of suspicion, fear and scorn.

THE CRUSADES

The first major encounter between East and West was the Crusades that could not have led to any just appreciation or even understanding of opponent's beliefs and ethical attitudes. The atmosphere in which wars are fought by its very nature inhibits any serious study and appreciation of

From a speech, given in Arabic on 11 October, 1963, at a meeting in the University of London, attended by a large number of students, teachers and scholars.

each other's religious and ethical concepts, and hardly allows mutual co-operation on an equal and honourable footing. But the spirit behind the Crusades was aroused only by making the Crusaders believe indiscriminately all kinds of impossible reports about the Muslims' beliefs and practices. Without their readiness to believe, for example, that the Muslims were pagan brutes, from whose clutches the Holy Land must be liberated, they would not have been so easily persuaded to make war. The Crusades did nevertheless, to some degree, reduce though not bridge the gulf between East and West.

COLONIALISM

A more direct and closer encounter took place in the nineteenth century when, for reasons political and economic, the West invaded the East. It brought with it everything it had — its civilisation and culture, science and technology, its systems of government and administration — everything, the good as well as the bad. The East, left long behind the West in its scientific and economic progress towards a more efficiently organised order of things, was dumbfounded by this onslaught: it was not in the right frame of mind to effectively understand the West or benefit from its achievements. Another factor that prevented appreciation of the West, let me say, was its own civilisation which had all the attributes of a civilisation whose religious impulse had atrophied. Moreover, the attitude of the Westerners was that they were the masters of the East. This attitude was compounded by a feeling of racial superiority manifested in individual behaviour as well as in general policies quite incompatible with human dignity and the spirit of democracy — ideas applauded by the Westerners, for which they had struggled exclusively in their own lands and exclusively for themselves. These policies could hardly assuage the injured feelings of those who till then were the rulers of the same lands.

One consequence of the West's impact on the East was the development among the Eastern peoples of an attitude of surrender, of abject subservience before Western values and ideas. The blind imitation of the West that accompanied this development inevitably robbed the peoples of the East of their distinctive personality and of their self-respect. Equally inevitably the West could not look upon the East with feelings of even equality, much less esteem or admiration; certainly it could not turn to the East for inspiration or guidance, nor for anything original or creative — an East that seemed to have faded away and dissolved into the civilisation of the West.

Most recently of all, the Eastern peoples have been absorbed by the idea of nationalism, imported from the West. The countries of the West had adopted it, turning away from the bond of the Roman Church; it aroused in them an enthusiasm which was almost 'religious' in nature. It is worthwhile observing here, though in parenthesis, that the West, having experienced the disaster and destruction generated by narrow-minded nationalism, is now retreating from this concept. But so deeply has nationalism taken root in the minds of the Eastern peoples who carry the torch of the Divine message, they dare not now imagine themselves helping the West with the light and guidance, they have, as they did in the past. Those custodians of the Divine message in its perfect and final form who could lead humanity towards a new world order of peace and happiness are now lost in the by-ways of nationalism, their sphere of effectiveness narrowed to limited geographical or linguistic or racial interests. They have sealed from mankind as a whole those rays of light destined to illumine the whole world which have always been the source of guidance.

ORIENTALISM

With the emergence of Orientalism it was expected that the gulf between East and West would be bridged, with fairness and justice; that the barriers between two families of mankind, resulting from ignorance or geographical remoteness would be lifted, and mutual understanding take their place. It was hoped that the Orientalists would be able to transmit to the West all the riches of the East — the teachings of the Prophets, the general moral values, the practical examples of the noble life set by the Prophets and by spiritual leaders, in the excellent code of laws and precepts for the guidance of human conduct.

True the Orientalists have many achievements to their credit, not least the rediscovery of many Islamic works long buried from the light of day. They collected, corrected and published manuscripts whose importance is impossible to deny. No-one who has any love of fairness or of learning will deny the scientific rigour and depth of their approach and their painstaking labours. But Muslims rightly feel that many of the Orientalists were inspired rather by religious and cultural prejudices than by scientific motives. They have therefore deeply disappointed the lovers of truth who expected from them greater immunity from emotional predilections and inherited prejudices, a greater interest in truth, a greater searching for the reality and, above all, a greater moral courage in acknowledging it. Orientalism has, alas, for all its apparent scientific method, failed to be genuinely scientific or bridge the gap between East and West. It has failed to give to the West what the soul of many a Westerner, disillusioned by the emptiness of a materialistic civilisation, has long been seeking, namely, a true and full picture of religion in general and of Islam in particular. I say of Islam in particular, because we Muslims believe it to be the last heavenly message to mankind and therefore a message of everlasting value. Islam embodies the teachings and wisdom of all earlier Divine revelations; it is in tune with the spirit of the age; it seeks to carry civilisation forward and not, as some religions do, backward; it, in fact, has a wonderful potential to free civilisation from rigid extremism and stagnation and to generate new moulds consistent with the spirit of its own teachings as well as the needs of our changing times.

THE GULF REMAINS

Crusades, colonialism, Orientalism — whatever the reasons, it is clear that East and West remain isolated from one another. Whenever the two came together it was in an atmosphere of mutual suspicion, even hatred. Seldom have they joined hands for the greater good of humanity and with a view to building an ideal civilisation. A readiness to exchange the natural capabilities and knowledge acquired through generations has been almost absent; exchange, if any, has taken place in a very restricted area.

THE 'PROPHETIC MISSION'

The peculiar temperament of the East leavened by religion, has been inspired, from time to time, by noble Prophets and ceaselessly nourished by spiritual movements and the teachings of religious leaders. The East has directed its genius to the study and the making of man, rather than the world external to him. It has sought the infinitude within man, to discover mysteries within him, to awaken the hidden capacities therein, to awaken inner forces which have no equal, to orientate man's tendencies and inclinations, for the reform and refinement of his morals, without which human life can have no sound basis.

All the Prophets of God that came and the last of the Prophets, Muhammad, peace be upon them all, made the making of a new man their sole concern.

They opened to man the infinite forces within. They awakened him to his hidden possibilities. They opened the eye of heart that he could see the Creator of this great universe and receive the treasures of light and life, knowledge, love and contentment, confidence and unity of moral purpose. They enabled man to know the real source of all life and order in the universe; to see the universe not as divided into many warring elements but as an integrated whole governed by one Omnipotent and Merciful Will, which does not discriminate between East and West: 'His, verily, is all creation and commandment. Blessed be God; the Lord of the Worlds' (*al-A'rāf*, 7: 54). And, says the Qur'ān further: 'The Lord of the East and of the West; there is no God save Him; so choose thou Him alone for thy Guardian' (*al-Muzzammil*, 73: 9).

The Prophets thus liberated man from all forms of idolatry and dualism, from superstition and subservience to irrational tradition and legend and from every submission except submission before the Creator and Ruler of the universe.

THE NEW MAN

Through the window to man's inner resources, the Prophets enabled him to see himself as the vicegerent of God in this world, in whom God had breathed a spark of His Divine spirit, to whom He gave knowledge, to whom He gave

31

the government of the world in His name, creating everything to serve man, and man to serve Him alone, trusting man with a sacred mission because he was created by God in the best of moulds such that He made the angels bow down before him, and thus forbade him thereafter to prostrate himself before any other creature. As God says: 'Surely We created man of the best stature' (*al-Tīn,* 95: 4) and 'We have honoured the children of Adam; provided them with transport on land and sea; given them for sustenance things good and pure, and conferred on them special favours, above a great part of Our creation' (*al-Isrā',* 17: 70).

Because of the Prophets' teachings, man saw the diverse peoples scattered through the length and breadth of the earth as a single family, originating from the same parents. In the light of the prophetic teaching mankind was one brotherhood, only that man being the most worthy of God's affection who was the most benevolent towards God's family. The diverse members of the human race were regarded as if members of one body, so that any feeling of pain in one member should be felt in another. The prophetic teachings made clear to man that all distinctions between the various members of the human family based upon colour, territory or nationality or material possessions, were a legacy from ignorance and barbarism; men listened when the Blessed Prophet, peace be upon him, said to the Lord in the darkness of the night — 'I bear witness that all creatures are brothers'; and they listened when, in the broad light of day, he proclaimed aloud before huge crowds of people: 'Oh men! all of you are from Adam, and Adam is from clay. There is no superiority for an Arab over a non-Arab; nor for a non-Arab over an Arab, nor for white over black, nor for black over white, except by virtue of piety'. As God says: 'Oh mankind, We have created you from a male and female, and made you into peoples and tribes in order that you may know one from another. Truly the most honourable among you in the sight of God is the most pious among you' (*al-Ḥujurāt,* 49: 13).

The Prophets of God who came and the last of the Prophets, Muhammad, peace be upon them all, were able to mobilise a potentiality in man that no branch of learning, neither philosophy nor psychology, could ever have done or can ever do. In fact these branches of learning have not been able even to comprehend the full extent of human potential. But the Prophets did not merely mobilise this potential, they mobilised it to a certain end — the good of the individual and the good of mankind as a whole. They aroused in man the desire to seek God's pleasure, to seek closeness with the Divine. They inspired him to love and obey God, and to love and serve God's creatures; to strive for their happiness and well-being even at the cost of one's own. They created in man the urge to bring his self to account in great depth and with meticulous detail. Their teachings discovered in man the potential for selfless love, for graciousness and delicacy of feeling, for compassion and imagination. They gave to him his greatest ideals — purity of soul, nobility of conduct, freedom from worldly success, and a sense of attainable sublimity. In sum, a new man is the greatest fruit of prophethood, the Prophets implanted in him a longing for God; their gifts to man were faith and knowledge of God, gifts available from no other source. Noble seeds they sowed; rich harvest they reaped.

PROPHETIC METHODOLOGY

These Prophets of the East did not concern themselves with discovering or exploiting the secrets of nature. They invented neither tools nor machinery; but pure intentions and noble pursuits they did create.

As for natural or material success, these depend upon human will and direction. Where man has a lofty cause to serve, with true sincerity and conviction, he does, even with little means, achieve such mighty results and render such invaluable service to mankind as even a very advanced technological civilisation cannot. When there is a strong and sincere will, the unknown is somehow discovered, resources become available or sufficient, somehow difficulties are overcome, and man makes a way for himself over seemingly insuperable obstacles.

By contrast, when there is no higher end in view to arouse genuine commitment, the greatest resources are wasted, and all the efforts of the toolmakers and the skilled labourers ultimately come to nothing. I have no wish to undermine knowledge or the instruments man has acquired to serve his ends, but would stress that these are not indispensable when compared with some of the most elementary and most powerful human urges. Consider a man dying for food or drink, or a mother when care for her child swells up in her, or any lover longing for what he loves — the very intensity of feeling compels a search for the means of satisfying it.

The Prophets sought to put before man the right kind of objectives, to draw from him the highest desire, the highest commitment. Once devotion to goodness and conviction are present, men do find ways of self-fulfilment. It was just this sincerity and intensity of desire that brought about the achievement of these noble objectives given to mankind in their most perfect form by the last of the Prophets. A civilisation was thus achieved out of very poor means indeed, a civilisation in which a man could live with honour and dignity and find comfort of mind and soul. To be sure this civilisation was of a relatively simple pattern, yet it contained great potential for growth and expansion in the future.

WESTERN CIVILISATION

Then came the West's turn — the age of Renaissance and discovery. At that time, for various reasons — the weakening of the hold of religious and moral values as a result of wrong and monopolistic conduct by the religious leaders, the economic and political pressures, the struggle for existence which the various European nations had gone through within the narrow boundaries of Europe, and all the attendant problems — the West turned its attention from man himself to the external world, from man as a spiritual entity to man as a physical structure; it turned from his heart and soul to the body of nature, to the sciences of physics, chemistry, astronomy, mathematics and so on. And it is God's law that He gives to every man that for which he strives: 'Of the bounties of the Lord We bestow freely on all — on these as well as those: the bounties of the Lord are not denied to anyone' (al-Isrā', 17: 20).

The West made great strides in the natural sciences, discovering the secrets of nature, one after the other,

34

achieving success after success, until its present level of attainment, hardly dreamt of in the past. This needs no elaboration, particularly here in this place which is rightly considered as one of the pioneers of modern learning and Western civilisation; and in this University, where I have the honour of addressing you, there has continued, as in so many other similar universities of Europe, the advance of modern science and the discovery of the means for these astounding achievements in the fields of science and technology which are a blessing from God, the value of which should not be underrated.

THE CONSEQUENCES
These resources were in the nature of a means, an instrument. They brought enormous wealth, power, energy — much less could remove the barriers between peoples and between individuals, establish brotherhood, secure at last a genuine world peace, and guarantee happiness to every human being. East and West could come closer. All the obstacles that were the result of man's poverty and weakness, that had plagued his life in the past, had gone. Machines and means enough existed for man to realise his objectives quickly and efficiently; there was no excuse whatsoever, none, for any seeker after virtue, any lover of humanity, for any standard-bearer of peace, there was no reason whatever for any individual, or society or state, to have failed.

But has the world been transformed into a natural paradise? Have we rid ourselves of fear, anxiety, warfare, enmity, poverty, disease? Have we banished hatred and tyranny? Have we established peace and the brotherhood of man? What need of an answer? This great city of London has witnessed two horrendous global wars and has been a victim of all the destruction and suffering consequent upon them. And, we all live in an age haunted by the spectre of nuclear war. Whole libraries of books recount for us the waywardness of this civilisation, the profound misery of those who live within or outside its wealth and power, they recount the failure of its morality, the loosening of social ties and the disintegration of family, the gathering tensions and anxieties, the predominance of fear, the terrible isolation, the feeling of having been betrayed and cast adrift.

What has brought about these results? The resources themselves can hardly be blamed. The instruments and machines produced by modern civilisation were as capable of being used for the good of mankind; since they have no will or direction of their own, the blame lies elsewhere.

FAITH, THE KEY

The answer is no secret, nor requires extraordinary intelligence. It is that man himself has not kept pace with the progress of technology; institutions and machines have developed, but not human motives and attitudes. Indeed, it could be said that the sciences have progressed at the expense of a commensurate progress in man himself, in man's morality, in his potential for the orientation of his tendencies and inclination towards a general good. Technology has advanced at the price of man's heart and soul. The West has directed its genius, its intelligence and will, to the external world, and away from man himself who is the very soul of this universe, the masterpiece of creation. And even when it paid any heed to man's inner self, its access was limited by a thick crust of materialism that made it impossible to reach the ground of man's inner reality, to really make contact with the very solid facts of the inner life, and so justly value faith and belief and morality. Likewise the West has shied away from the source that guides man and inspires him towards goodness: his *heart,* upon the soundness of which rests the soundness of his whole life.

Unfortunately, even if the West wished to discover the secret to the world of the heart and guide humanity by it, it could not do so. For there is a special key which opens the doorway to man's inner treasures. And however impressive the industries of the West may be, however fine their products and however great the genius of the peoples of the West, they are incapable of making that key or breaking the lock, for it is not like the lock of banks and factories; it is a spiritual lock, whose only key is 'faith'; that key was gifted to humanity by Prophets, which has been lost, or lies buried beneath the dreary weight of modern civilisation or under the ruins of houses of worship.

FAITH AND SCIENCE

The affliction of humanity lies in the separation of the West from the East, in the separation of science from faith, a separation which has proved disastrous for mankind. Faith had been making strides and growing for long ages in the East, while in more recent centuries, science has been making strides and growing in the West. And faith continues to wait for the companionship of science, while science stands lost in need of the guidance of faith. Humanity is waiting for the two to come together and co-operate in order to produce a new generation; and there can be no hope of peace and true happiness without this blessed co-operation between faith and science.

THE CALL TO THE WEST

As for the East, my friends of the West, its wealth does not consist of 'oil', the black gold which you transport to your respective countries and then use to run planes and cars. Its real wealth is that faith which sprang up and blossomed there. You already benefited from some of this wealth at the beginning of your Christian era. Then again, in the opening decades of the seventh century A.D., the same treasure of wealth gushed forth in the desert of Arabia, and burst thence with a force and speed unprecedented in human history. From a remote valley in Arabia, it reached in no time to the farthest ends of the then known world, showering its blessings everywhere, enriching every part of the world so that there blossomed forth everywhere a new life. It can still be appropriated and made use of. It is still capable of overcoming all the problems that confront our modern civilisation; it can inject into it fresh vigour and a new vitality by providing a new sense of purpose, by reorienting the instruments and institutions of science and technology. This alone can lead to the making of a new society, the dawn of a new age. Upon you, who belong to this great country, lies a great responsibility, for you were the pioneers of modern world civilisation, and your national life is still energetic, still full of creative possibility. You can inaugurate a new era, set human history on a new course.

Hearken the Qur'ān: 'There hath come to you from God a

37

new Light and a perspicuous Book — wherewith God guideth all who seek His pleasure to ways of peace and safety, and leadeth them out of darkness by His Will, into the Light, and guideth them to a path that is straight.' (*al-Mā'ida*, 5: 15-16).

Chapter Two

The Barriers of Pride and Arrogance

*What prevents the West from responding positively to the
guidance offered by the Prophets of God, most of whom
appeared in the East, the final embodiment of their teachings
being Islam as brought by the last of them, Muhammad, may
Allah bless all of them?*

*Nadwi identifies pride and arrogance as the major reasons.
First the Greeks, then the Romans: each in turn attained great
heights of intellectual and material progress, each followed
the path of decay and degeneration, each was offered the
prophetic guidance, each rejected the hand extended to it for
it appeared from a world which they considered to be
barbarous. The same story was repeated after the advent of
the Prophet Muhammad, peace be upon him, in the sixth
century. He breathed new life into the decaying human
culture of the time and established the socio-religious order
which was the common heritage of humanity. It was
unfortunate that when the same Islam, though weakened in
spirit, reached Europe — in Spain and Sicily — it was
rejected and its traces were barbarically erased. Thus Europe
never received the true message of the Prophets, with the
result that its entire progress took place in a wrong
framework.*

*The advances in science and technology made by the West
have obviously placed increasing powers in the hands of man,
but not the ability to use them properly. The nations of the
East are blindly following the West and are prey to the same
diseases. But, says Nadwi, there is no other panacea for the
ills of mankind; any nation, whether Eastern or Western,
may come forward and embrace the Divine guidance and
hold its banner aloft.* [Ed.]

2

There is a story — perhaps you know it — of a high-caste Raja who very nearly drowned while bathing. He was rescued by a man of very low birth who, seeing the Raja's plight, promptly dived in and brought him safely to the bank. Naturally the Raja wanted to know the rescuer's name. However, when he realised the man's low caste he was deeply incensed and ordered the man severely punished for defiling him by his unholy touch. The man was duly punished and made an example of. Now it happened that the Raja found himself drowning again in the same river and, by coincidence, the same low-born man saw him. This time, however, the man did not act promptly; he reflected instead on the punishment he had received before. He might easily have rescued the Raja but dared not do so, and the high-born noble Raja lost his life in consequence.

Now you may think this story exaggerated — but there is nothing in it so incredible if you take into account the oddities of the human mind. Family pride and self-conceit have drowned many individuals, many peoples — so blinded by prejudice that they would rather face extinction than accept help or advice from someone they regard, through force of tradition or simply racial arrogance, as inferior. There are many examples of this in the moral and religious history of mankind — one may find the pattern even now in the attitude of the civilised, progressive nations of the world. No, the story of the Raja is no mere fable — it tells a truth and expresses one of the underlying causes of the death of nations.

THE GREEK CIVILISATION
Who has not heard the name of Greece, birthplace of

From an article in Urdu written in 1949, and published in the Daily Ta'mīr *of Lucknow, later rendered into Arabic and published in* Al-Muslimūn *of Damascus.*

world-famous philosophers, poets and scientists? Socrates, Plato, Aristotle — the land was abundant with intellectual genius and its people provided with every resource to make it great and prosperous. In its day of glory it was the fountainhead of all the creative arts that require human ingenuity and intellectual refinement. Other nations prided themselves upon being the disciples of Greek successes in philosophy, in science, in poetry and drama, in mathematics, sculpture, architecture, in the sciences of government.

Yet, for all this, there is so much more that does not fall within the domain of human reason: the mysteries of life — the origin, duration, meaning of Creation, immortality and its relation to mortality, the nature and relation of good and evil, of lawful and unlawful. Such questions Greek reason could not and did not deal with — they are beyond hairsplitting logic, beyond unaided human intellect. The Greeks treated them at best with poetic fancies, and with serious consequences. They attributed to God frailties that would shame even human beings and that made God ineffective in questions of man's ethical and social conduct. They rationalised primitive mythology, sanctifying a chaotic hierarchy of gods and goddesses whose lusts and passions made love and fear of God impossible. The moral and religious life of the Greeks degenerated, accepted standards of good and evil conduct lost all authority. Philosophical reasoning was used to morally justify every act of treachery, lust or sensuality — thus, reasons were advanced to explain the need and benefits of prostitution.

Finally, this famous land of philosophers, poets, scientists, fell victim to the moral chaos it had itself generated, and the lamp of learning was extinguished.

Just at the time when Greek civilisation had reached its last stages of decadence, there arose, in the lands to the southeast of Greece and among a people known to be intellectually backward, men who came to be called Prophets of God. These men were not philosophers, nor poets, nor mathematicians, but inspired by faith and armed with Divine guidance. They possessed a knowledge, vouchsafed them by God, of the mysteries of life, and of the certainty of final human destiny fulfilled in the life to come. What the Greeks

41

possessed was by contrast a tangled web of knowledge more and more difficult to unravel as time passed — they played with the pebbles on the seashore of knowledge while the Prophets traversed the currents and discovered the pearls of the sea. The Greeks knew everything except *themselves* — they had no knowledge of how to encourage a single human being towards piety and purity, no knowledge of God, the Creator and Sustainer of the world. Greek civilisation stagnated in a chaos of intellectual rootlessness and bodily lusts. The Prophets of the East were by contrast a dynamic force — whoever was touched by their teaching felt himself become morally and spiritually purer, freed from the domination of desire. The Greeks' philosophy helped not a single individual to withstand his own desires and follow a virtuous life: the Prophets offered no book-learning whatsoever, but their teaching enabled their followers to triumph over every temptation of their lower selves, to reach the highest pinnacle of humanity.

The Prophets offered their guidance to the Greeks, without asking for any reward, but were rejected with scorn — how could an illiterate people, utterly ignorant of her arts and sciences, help Greece? That is how her very knowledge became a millstone round her neck; her civilisation rotted with the poison of godlessness; her strength sapped, and she finally tottered to ruins. The Qur'ān draws a vivid image:

> For when their apostles
> Came to them
> With clear signs, they exulted
> In such knowledge (and skill)
> As they had; but
> That very (wrath) at which
> They were wont to scoff
> Hemmed them in. (*Al-Mu'min,* 40: 83)

THE ROMAN CIVILISATION

The same fate overtook Rome, the political and intellectual heir of Greece. It surpassed Greece in the external organisation of society, in the art of constitution-making, in political administration and the techniques of warfare. Its extensive empire comprised all three continents of Europe,

Asia and Africa; in its day of glory it had no equal for political and military might, or for advancement of the technologies of building, sculpture, painting. But Rome too declined. Like Greece it failed to penetrate the real mysteries of life; it drew no inspiration from the vital message of the Prophets. Rome delighted in idolatry and the worship of human gods; its life became weighed down by extravagance, luxury, love of pleasure for its own sake, economic exploitation of class by class, so much so that the cruel perversions of gladiatorial sports, of flagellation of slaves, and crucifixion of innocent men and women came to be looked upon as noble arts.

A great many Prophets of God were born, at this time, in the eastern territories of the empire. The fame of their teaching spread to Rome where the men of power scorned to hear them. The Romans believed themselves to be born rulers — how should they then bring themselves to follow those who were their subjects and slaves? Their argument was time born, explains the Qur'ān:

> If (this Message) were
> A good thing, (such men)
> Would not have gone
> To it first, before us. (al-Aḥqāf, 46: 11)

The Romans heeded not the Prophets. Their national self-conceit and arrogance produced the evils of immorality, self-indulgence and anarchy which drowned their civilisation:

> That was because there
> Came to them apostles
> With clear signs,
> But they said:
> 'Shall (mere) human beings
> Direct us?' So they rejected
> (The Message) and turned away
> But God can do without (them)
> And God is
> Free of all needs,
> Worthy of all praise. (al-Taghābun, 64: 6)

THE SIXTH CENTURY WORLD
In the sixth century, Rome, Persia, China and India were

43

the most civilised countries of the world, but rot had set in in every root and branch of human life. The lamps of guidance lit by the great Prophets burnt dimly and were on the point of extinction. Science and learning were devoid of the inspiration of faith and of the true knowledge of God. Religion and culture were under the sway of superstition and hypothetical conjectures and, in politics, social life and morality, human desires had full and unrestricted play. Both kingship and priesthood had become vehicles of exploitation. Churches, synagogues, temples — all had abdicated the leadership of mankind to Satan. Christianity, Zorastrianism and Hinduism had all lost their spiritual glow. These religions had become incapable of creating among the masses or the intellectuals any desire for moral purity, dutifulness and genuine love and fear of God. They lacked clear-cut principles on the basis of which a healthy social or collective edifice could be raised.

In Persia and Rome more and more taxes and fines made the life of the poor miserable and they became so completely absorbed in the cares and anxieties of everyday existence that they could give no thought to the deeper problems of life. The middle classes had been completely corrupted by the desire for more and more wealth and by an insatiable craving to model their lives upon those of the richer classes. Life had become so costly and their living standards had risen so high that the Persian nobles paid out thousands of gold coins to purchase a single head-gear. In their dress, diet and household adornments the Persians had gone to the last extreme of luxury and refinement.

In India caste-divisions were becoming even more rigid and the natural differences between man and man were increased a thousand-fold by artificial distinctions. Sexual immorality invaded not only the literature of the land but also the temples and sacred houses of worship. Wealth and power became the sole objects of human endeavour. Religion was reduced to a few meaningless rituals and philosophic wranglings.

In short, the civilised nations of the world lay prostrate under the benumbing weight of their own culture and had lost all capacity to receive the Divine guidance and make it the goal of their lives.

THE ADVENT OF THE PROPHET

God in His wisdom chose for the spiritual regeneration of humanity a people who, though idolatrous and not far behind other nations in their immoralities, were yet free from the evils created by a highly artificial civilisation, by the wealth and power and by slavery to a far-flung empire. From among this people God chose a person distinguished by his noble heritage and unique for his extraordinary qualities of wisdom, courage, large-heartedness and capacity for leadership. He proved by the success of his missionary efforts, by his perseverance and toil, by his moral purity and spiritual greatness, that no one among all mankind was better fitted to shoulder the immense burden of prophethood.

Mankind had grown to maturity and the course of the world pointed clearly to the fact that it could no longer remain divided into racial and national compartments. Accordingly, Muhammad, the Prophet of God, peace be upon him, gave to the world a social and religious order complete in its details, clear in its outlines, that provides conclusively for the needs of all nations in the world, all classes among the nations, all individuals in the different classes and the circumstances of each individual's life; it offers adequate guidance to the poor as well as the rich, the rulers as well as the ruled, the young as well as the old, the civilised as well as the uncivilised, the high intellectuals as well as the unlettered and uneducated masses. In the social-religious order that he established, each individual is afforded the right and opportunity to develop to the utmost of his capacity and to achieve within human limits, the highest spiritual progress. No divisions of race, nationality and historical periods are admitted in this framework which contains within itself metaphysical tenets as well as well-defined and clear-cut principles and laws for the regulation of human needs. These laws are generous enough not to require amendments or additions.

Moreover, the system of life brought by the Prophet Muhammad, peace be upon him, contains not only important legal precepts and social laws, it provides adequate

45

spiritual motives for their observance and powerful psychological deterrents against their neglect. And his teachings are backed by the highest force of personal example and a life of dynamic activity lived in accordance with them.

THE ISLAMIC ORDER

This socio-religious order was the common heritage of all humanity, every nation and every land having an equal share therein. It gave an equal chance to all peoples to achieve the maximum of progress: no nation or race was singled out as having a monopoly. God clearly declared: 'We have divided you into tribes and families that you may be distinguished from each other; the highest and most respectable in the sight of God is he who is most God-fearing' (al-Ḥujurāt, 49: 13). The Prophet himself explained: Each one of you is descended from Adam and Adam was made of clay. The Arabs have no superiority over the non-Arabs nor the non-Arabs over the Arabs except on grounds of piety and moral purity.

In the early period of Islam we find Salmān of Persia, Suhaib of Rome and Bilāl of Abyssinia and their several compatriots working side by side with the Quraish of Makka and the Ansārs of Madina. We hear a great Caliph like 'Umar address Bilāl, the black Abyssinian, as 'our chief and leader'. Even later in the history of Islam we find new Muslims and Persians occupying the seats of religious learning in the cities and centres of knowledge of the Islamic world, offering guidance to the Arab chiefs and Muslims who had inherited Islam from their forefathers, and it is known for a fact that their verdicts commanded universal respect and obedience. Once Abdul Malik, a famous Umayyad Caliph, enquired of a traveller the names of the religious heads and distinguished men of learning in the great cities of Islam. He was surprised to learn that only in one city, the highest position among men of learning had gone to an Arab. In all other places non-Arab slaves or men descended from non-Arab slaves, occupied the highest seats of learning. On the occasion of Ḥajj, the greatest international gathering of Muslims, when the people from the whole Muslim world come together at one place, it was proclaimed that no one else except 'Atā bin Abī Ribāḥ, a freed slave, was competent to deliver judgements on disputed questions.

The whole history of Islam furnishes ample evidence to show that Islam gave equal and unfettered opportunities of development to men of diverse nationalities and races who accepted its message and joined its ranks and it elevated them without the slightest distinction of race or nationality and on this basis was fulfilled the prophecy of the Qur'ān about the Prophet Muhammad, peace be upon him, in respect of the oppressed and downtrodden people — he urges them to do good and prohibits them from evil-doing. He makes clean things lawful unto them and makes unlawful unto them things which are unclean and he removes from them the fetters and burdens which weigh them down (al-A'rāf, 7: 157). They tasted the sweetness of life for the first time and they achieved progress in all directions. Politically they founded kingdoms and empires, intellectually they added to the treasure-house of learning.

RELIGION AND EUROPEAN MISFORTUNE

Islam spread to Europe through Spain and flourished there for nearly eight hundred years. The Arabs of Spain suffered from many shortcomings. They were certainly far behind the Companions of the Prophet, peace be upon him, in religious sincerity and missionary fervour, still Europe had a splendid opportunity during the Arab rule over Spain to study the principles and laws of Islam through the writings of Spanish Muslims and examine its characteristics as a new social order. But Europe missed this opportunity owing to its religious prejudices and racial pride, two peculiarities which have always marked it and which it has received from ancient Greece and Rome as its emotional heritage. The people of Europe always looked upon Spanish Muslims as their political enemies. They did learn science and philosophy from them but took no notice of what was really valuable in their social life, until at last in a frenzy of religious prejudice and blind hostility they drove the Muslims out of Spain towards the African continent and then set out to efface, in a spirit of barbaric vandalism, all traces of their religious and cultural life from their country — this, even though Islamic culture had greatly enriched their own lives. They succeeded in

47

exiling Islam from the country where it had showered its innumerable blessings.

This vandalism delayed the Western renaissance by several centuries and when it did come at last, it started within the wrong framework, within mistaken conceptions about human life and destiny. As a result, Europe itself and the whole world of which it has become the intellectual leader was plunged into godlessness, moral anarchy and the pursuit of material desires and comforts. Europe had received no real light and no true guidance from religion. It was led by a few superstitions, prejudices and certain commentaries and interpretations of Christian scholars. The latter had compiled a whole world geography and an ecclesiastical world history which clashed with scientific discoveries and the latest advances in knowledge.

A stable and virtuous civilisation can be built only on a right conception of God, His attributes, the necessity of Divine revelation and its role in ordering human affairs and a view of life which shows man his right place in the total scheme of life. These things were totally strange to the European mind and a perverted Christianity, concerned only with the preservation of the spiritual and temporal power of the Church, insistent on the absolute veracity of the geographical and physical references in the scriptures, could hardly offer effective guidance.

Europe, in short, had never had the opportunity to understand and realise what a real religion can be like. If it had known real religion, the conflict between science and religion could have been avoided and all its evil consequences. So long as Islam was dominant in Spain, there was still a chance for Europe to realise the value of religion as a society-shaping power. But having missed it, through its blindness and prejudice, Europe had no alternative but to fall back on Christianity as the sole representative of religion, and Christianity in the form in which it then existed gave a totally false idea of religion. It made no distinction between the eternal values of life and the readjustments needed in social affairs owing to the change of circumstances. The standard-bearers of Christianity stood in the way of every intellectual advance and scientific progress, because they stuck to the old commentaries. They even went so far as to inflict severe punishments upon the new scientists and philosophers who repudiated old notions such as the movement of the sun round the earth. In consequence of their intellectual obscurantism and terrorism, men of light and learning all over Europe rebelled against religion and started their scientific investigations and philosophical speculation in complete indifference, nay blind opposition, to all religion and morality.

THE CONSEQUENCES

This wrong start in the field of knowledge produced many undesirable consequences. It made the progress of Western enlightenment aimless; lost in unravelling the maze of nature, unable to reach its Creator. European sciences missed the higher and more ultimate realities of knowledge. They did, no doubt, discover innumerable new facts and bring forward an imposing array of scientific truths; but failed to synthesise them into a purposeful, life-giving whole. This knowledge could offer no guidance to humanity in search of righteous living. Deprived of religious guidance, it lost self-discipline and moral sense. The new sciences achieved victory after victory in the field of knowledge, but left humanity in deeper moral darkness than they found it in.

The increase of knowledge meant an increase of powers in the hands of individuals and communities, but there was nothing in the life of the new civilisation to control these fast-growing powers. Man has become a giant of physical resources but in his passions and emotions remains a child, and in his inclinations and predilections, a follower of the devil. He has obtained control of the air, steam and electricity, of the innumerable forces of nature, but remains ignorant of and indifferent to the forces of virtue and righteousness and the objective of a good, healthy and balanced life, for these things can come only from a particular type of religious training which is anathema to the modern mind. Man is wasting his powers and resources either on trivial objects which are useful to humanity only in the narrowest sense or in destructive savageries fatal to himself and the civilisation he has built. National selfishness dominates the scene in Europe leading to national and class conflicts which destroy the lives and happiness of millions of human beings. Not content with this, Europe and America are now planning for a global war in which atomic weapons may annihilate everything human.

All the scientific discoveries of Europe, all its stupendous knowledge, will prove useless without the guidance of religion. There is much that is useful in this knowledge for certain narrow objectives but, on the whole, it does not give us those governing principles on which a healthy corporate existence can be built. Europe has solved many complex questions and answered many difficult enquiries about processes of the external physical universe, but the complex problems of its own life still defy solution and become every day more complex, more tangled and more difficult of solution.

ISLAM IS THE ANSWER

There is now only one way for the salvation of the Western world and that is to acknowledge its moral and intellectual failure as far as the ultimate issues of life and the guiding framework for social and corporate existence are concerned, and to turn to religion and prophetic revelation for the necessary guidance. Only a religion that gives the Western nations a right conception of God, of His attributes and His means; that inspires the Western mind with love and fear of Him; that awakens the soul without weakening intellect; that creates strong faith in an after-life when man will be held to account for all his deeds, secret or open, that provides, in the example of the Prophet's life, peace be upon him, and works (recorded in meticulous detail by reliable observers and historians), a substantial and practical guidance in every area of life — only such a religion can prevent the collapse from within of European civilisation.

But perhaps this will not be religion in the Western sense of the word, rather a complete social order whose actual working has been exemplified in the lives of millions of human beings belonging to different periods of history and in conformity with which the administration and governments of many countries and empires have been run. This religion will be free from the monasticism of Christianity, the materialism of the modern West, the yogic beliefs and practices of ancient India, the luxurious living of the ancient Persians, the softness and aesthetic excesses of the Greeks and the harsh rigours of the stoic philosophers. It should repudiate nationalism and stress the essential unity of all nations, races and classes. It should make man less selfish and free him from the domination of desire and thereby harness his energies to the constructive tasks of civilisation.

This kind of teaching with all the qualities I have enumerated is still extant in the Qur'ān, the only religious book free from human interpolation and alive in all its first purity. It can still put new life into the nations of the world, its inexhaustible intellectual wealth is still to hand and capable of facing the problems of modern times. The Qur'ān's profundity of thought remains accessible to general human understanding without the aid of laboured interpretations.

Likewise the Prophet's life, peace be upon him, and the wisdom of his teachings are applicable to all, covering a variety of situations and problems. For rich or poor, for young and old, for husbands or fathers, for wives or daughters, for the rulers and the ruled, for the treaty-maker or the sovereign at war — the Qur'ān and the life of Muhammad, peace be upon him, provide a store of principles and norms by which even the vastly altered conditions of modern life can be enriched and guided towards an equitable social order that really does permit to all men opportunity for fulfilment.

For the Western nations to turn to Islam requires enormous moral courage, it requires an admission of failure — and this precisely stands in the way of their taking the right path. The men in power in the West would rather see nations destroyed, landscapes and resources devastated, the whole of humanity plunged into distress, than make the admission. A false sense of prestige, inflated pride in their scientific and material progress, prevents them turning to the life-work of that unlettered Prophet, peace be upon him, who alone offers the hope of salvation. The result of this self-conceit is that generations of mankind face the possible destruction of all

51

existence.

And in the nations of Asia that are following in the footsteps of the European nations, there are the same, if not worse, problems. They too lack the spiritual reserves which alone can liberate human beings from the enslavement of desire. The great teachings of the Prophets, peace be upon them, had here showered their blessings but are now a spent force because of studied negligence — perverted and deformed by the over-refined debates of scholars and the logic-chopping of philosophers. Moreover, the peoples of the East lack the sense of national solidarity and the consciousness of citizenship, prevalent in the West, even though they have assumed the great burdens of ruling themselves. They cannot rise above petty selfish ends, and social and moral evils go unchecked: for example, social diseases like bribery, corruption and partisanship, have assumed enormous proportions that before operated in a relatively contained sphere.

WORSHIP OF THIS WORLD

However, these are only the symptoms of a much deeper sickness — excessive love, even worship, of this life. When individuals and nations fall to this sickness, states and empires decay and disintegrate, nations are enslaved or subjugated, brother plots against brother, treachery, cruelty, greed become the norms of conduct. Modern education seems rather to feed than cure this sickness. The only cure is to inspire men with a sincere faith in God, in the accountability of man for his actions in the life to come.

It is true that all nations have produced great men, poets or philosophers, scholars, soldiers, statesmen, heroes, and their history does not lack examples of great selfishness, splendid sincerity and sacrifice: there are noble traditions of loyalty, patriotism, love of liberty. And these must be preserved by the governments and peoples concerned for they are a precious heritage. But they are plainly insufficient as a guiding and ennobling force in the complexities of man's collective life and the general shaping of human destinies. It is only the teachings of the Prophets of God, above all of the Prophet Muhammad, peace be upon them all, that can rescue us (as they did fourteen hundred years ago) from social and moral decadence and the threat of total annihilation. Those teachings, fortunately, have been preserved intact by his followers.

For the nations of Asia, the Qur'ān and the teachings of Muhammad, peace be upon him, are easier of access, but they have no monopoly. Just as in the past, the Seljuki and then the Ottoman Turks assumed the leadership of the Muslim world and replaced the Arabs as the champions of Islam, so it is equally open to any modern nation to adopt the teachings of the Prophet, peace be upon him, and become the spearhead of a new movement and the spiritual leader of mankind in place of the present-day Muslims who seem to have lost the spirit of those teachings.

If any of your children or those whom you hold dear suffers from illness or disease you go to every doctor or physician and do not confine your efforts to any particular system of medicine. You have an open mind and examine with absolute impartiality the claims of every alternative method of treatment. The same impartiality and open-mindedness should be extended to rival theories of life and competing socio-religious orders by those who are presiding over the destinies of an ailing civilisation or guiding the affairs of particular nations which suffer from social and moral weakness of a dangerous nature. Surely the responsibilities of national and international leaders are much greater than those of individuals who have to look after diseased and sick loved ones. If the latter can rise above their personal likes and dislikes in order to save the lives of their dear ones, those at the helm of affairs should be much more open-minded and catholic in the search for social cures with a view to bringing salvation, peace and stability to their peoples. What the Holy Qur'ān said to the peoples of the sixth century is as valid in the twentieth, and as urgent:

> Light and guidance has come to you from God. Those who desire to earn the pleasure of God are shown the way of peace and safety by the Qur'ān and such people are taken out by God from darkness into light and led to the right path. (al-Mā'ida, 5: 15-16)

Chapter Three

The Message to Germany

Why not Germany, asks Nadwi?

Germany occupies a special place among the nations of Europe because of some of its outstanding qualities as well as the intellectual contributions it has made to European civilisation. It has been a land of restless revolutionaries — like Martin Luther (d. 1546), Immanuel Kant (d. 1804), Friedrich Nietzsche (d. 1900), Karl Marx (d. 1883). At the same time the German nation has exhibited human qualities of self-confidence, innovation and industry. It has also fought two world wars in an unsuccessful bid for world leadership.

Yet Germany also failed to chart out a course different from that of Western civilisation in general. It made no attempt to create a new man, or a new society. If it had, it could have easily attained the leadership of mankind.

The failure of Germany must be viewed in the perspective of the history of religion in Europe. It received a version of Christianity which subscribed to the dogmas of incarnation and vicarious atonement. It saw the representatives of this religion acting in morally degenerate ways and suppressing the advance of science and knowledge. The result has been a conflict between science and religion, exclusion of religion from public affairs and a general indifference to it. On the other hand, Europe also remained estranged from Islam for reasons explained earlier. One important factor has been the confrontation that Europe had with the Ottomans. No doubt the Turks gave a new impetus to Islam, but some of their actions in Europe can hardly be justified from an objective Islamic criteria.

The world today faces a void and a great danger. Who, among the nations of the world, shall come forward and hold the torch of Islam? [Ed.]

55

3

OUTSTANDING CHARACTERISTICS

The German nation has for centuries enjoyed a remarkable reputation for courage and adventurousness, together with sobriety of thought, pragmatism and untiring industry. It has produced a great number of outstanding personalities whose moral and intellectual achievements have left a lasting impression upon the philosophy and conduct of Western society. To illustrate this let me briefly recall three men from this great number, each of whom founded a distinctive school of thought.

First, Martin Luther. Luther directed his energies to the Bible with a view to reformation in the Church as it then existed; he preached passionately for containment of the unlimited rights and powers enjoyed by the Pope and the priests. The mark he left upon Christianity has proved indelible: he is known, and rightly, as the founder of a religion — Protestantism. Secondly, Immanuel Kant, the philosopher whose profound *Critique of Pure Reason* laid bare the limitation of human reason, reducing the whole work of the rationalists to a heap of ruins. Kant has been justly described as God's greatest gift to this country. Thirdly, I name in my list, Nietzsche, a radically unorthodox thinker who, in revolt against the prevailing intellectual system (largely Christian) waged a life-long battle against the beliefs and assumptions, and the philosophies, current in his time.

Each of these schools of thought or movements showed the revolutionary boldness, the restless originality and capacity for profound change, that are basic and characteristic elements in the make-up of the German people. These movements were revolutionary in the real sense — at times

---

From a speech made at the Engineering University of Berlin on Saturday, 14 October, 1964, attended by the University teachers, students and people from other walks of life.

their influence was limited and faint, but often very extensive, profound and clearly defined. Revolutionary outlook and intellectual restlessness were embodied at the highest level in the person of Karl Marx — a man whose thought led to what is considered the greatest rebellion against the existing (but archaic) systems of the present age, and whose thought still nourishes restlessness in a very large part of the world.

The German people have been justly famed too for their intense urge to attain a leading place among the world's nations, for their great self-confidence. The last two World Wars were, at bottom, a restless revolutionary adventure into the sphere of world politics and domination. Even today this nation is fired by optimism, by the need to satisfy through solid achievements its immense capacity for creative work. Germany could not otherwise have survived the disasters it has experienced over the first fifty or so years of this century, disasters that have few parallels in history. Where most nations would have been paralysed by absolute defeat, the German people have more than survived — out of the debris of World War II they have reconstructed and revived a vigorous social, industrial and aesthetic life.

SHORTCOMINGS

However, neither the adventures and experiences of this mighty nation, nor the revolutionary movements initiated by it could bring notable changes except within limited circles. Germany has undeniably played an important part in the orientation of European thought and the evolution of Western society. But it could not totally transform the basic religious trends in Europe, nor could it repair and renovate the common man's way of thinking or living. It failed to set up a new and healthy society, to create a new and better world. The two wars were fought for worldly objectives — not for the sake of the purification of Christianity, nor for the sake of high moral values, nor for the establishment of humanistic principles; nor was their objective the wresting of leadership from the tyrant and unrighteous and its transfer to the just and merciful — they were not waged to stamp out sin, vice, lewdness and inhumanity. I may be excused if I say that, in fact, they were fought for the sole purpose of wresting power and supremacy: both the contestants seemed to agree that injustice, tyranny, aggression and spoliation might continue undisturbed but exclusively under its own supervision and guidance.

Given their eminent position among the world's nations, one wonders, might not the German people have aimed rather at bringing about a world revolution more extensive and far-reaching in its effect than that which has been achieved by all past turmoils? A revolution to benefit not Germany only, not Europe only, but the whole of mankind? A revolution aimed at bringing about genuine world peace, and healthy and creative change? How more valuable such a revolution would have been had the distinguished leaders of Germany brought it about.

In spite of its setbacks Germany is abreast of the rest of Europe, perhaps even ahead of it — certainly in terms of resourcefulness, of inventiveness in the ambition to produce the amenities of life, Germany is giving the lead to its neighbours. But in the present order of things, its use of the remarkable intelligence and genius of her people, their technical skill and perfection, their sense of discipline and perseverance, has been restricted to serving this ambition. While it is true that Germany has outpaced her neighbours in industrial development, in international trade and commercial strength, yet, of Germany one might have expected more.

THE UNREALISED POSSIBILITIES

One might have expected that this nation, which has ever been a cradle and home of revolutionary thinkers, might rebel against a civilisation that has converted man into a wayward, destructive being, a civilisation in which man is adapted to the machine and in process of becoming a machine — deaf and blind, heartless and soulless, lacking either belief or conscience. In this civilisation the entire world is becoming a vast gambling hall for quick risks and quick profits, and for human souls a vast slaughterhouse. It recognises only trade and commerce as its objectives and so has rendered life void of its real joy, of variety with depth of appreciation.

One might have hoped that Germany might resist a civilisation in which life has been reduced to pointless moving hither and thither, to constant anxiety amid a general competitiveness that is both fruitless and aimless. Deprived of his most precious and noble attributes — faith, sincerity and purity of thought, depth and simplicity of desire, humanity — what is man? What is he, if not a blindfolded bullock tethered to a machine, stupefied and spiritually dying?

It was no idle hope that some European nation, but most especially Germany, should reverse the ideologies and artificial values that have so debased man, and bring about a change, not only in their own land, but throughout the world. These ideologies and values though man-made are yet deeply revered — as though divine in origin — but they have robbed man of his serenity, sapped and side-tracked his resourcefulness, and quite destroyed his real freedom.

The German people, whose true worth has never been rightly appreciated by their European neighbours, who have always been envied, distrusted and unequally treated by them, have nevertheless served the same ideology and for the same goal — material success, that too, with their special genius and phenomenal efficiency. Germany has not, as perhaps it alone could, tried to break the artificial and narrow bounds within which Europe has been living for centuries. It has not tried to take that great leap forward to change its own destiny and that of the world and to secure for itself the leadership of the world. Germany might have opened a new chapter in world history by altogether freeing mankind of the old and the new — the oriental and the occidental — ways of life and thought, and thus rescued the world from the desperate consequences of materialism to which science, adapted to the service of technology, has committed mankind. Compared to this, the achievements of all the revolutionary leaders and thinkers (whether in economics or sociology or politics) would have paled into insignificance.

RELIGION IN EUROPE

It is puzzling and incomprehensible that Europe with all its dynamism, Europe which is full of life's good things, which leads the majority of the civilised world, which has opened up the natural universe, harnessed matter and energy to its service — it is puzzling that such a Europe, stranger to a static or inactive life, should be associated with a religious system that (while preaching humanism) believes in an intermediary between man and his Creator and subscribes to the principle of vicarious atonement in the crucifixion of Christ. It is puzzling because this is a dogma that belittles the worthiness of action and effort and thereby undermines will and activity, initiative and achievement.

To cap it all, representatives of this religion acted for a long time as barriers between the inquisitive, ambitious, dynamic people of Europe and the realms of knowledge and discursive reason. Deviations from the theories advanced by the commentators of the Bible and from the teachings of the clergy, were considered heretical. Persons who in the light of their own commonsense, observations and experience gave vent to their opinion in any way differently from those of the commentators or the clergy were persecuted with a cruelty unparalleled in the history of any other religion.

In course of time Europe rose against the bigotry and narrow-mindedness of the Church and resisted the unjustified persecution: it burst all the restraints that had imprisoned it and then advanced materially to an extent before undreamt of. Great strides were made in the arts and literature, in the natural and social sciences. The effort exhausted Europe mentally and physically — it lost that balance which is the mainspring of the genuine well-being of man, and adopted that extreme materialism of outlook which, with the passage of time, has become its second nature. The Church retains even today some sort of sway over many Western countries but, by and large, a European's attitude towards religion is divorced from all reason and commonsense, and in matters relating to civilisation and culture he acts quite independently of it. This separation and contradiction between belief and action is the essential feature of every step he makes towards progress and of every facet of his way of living.

EUROPE AND ISLAM

Apart from this contradiction, the fact that Europe remained a stranger to Islam, a religion with uncompromised monotheism as its basis and clear-cut beliefs, distinguished for its simplicity, practicability, dynamism, self-confidence and respect for human endeavour, has been an event of tragic significance. In the scale of values of this religious system, the individual's effort and action occupy a very high place; so much so, that according to its cardinal articles of faith, they are the basis of reward or retribution, both in this life and the Hereafter. According to Islam, this life is but a bridge to cross over to the next world; thus inspiring a man to develop the qualities of disciplined manliness and dedication to high-minded ideals. Europe remained oblivious to the Apostle of this Divine message about whom the Qur'ān in its inimitable and majestic style says: he is 'the Prophet who can neither read nor write, whom they will find inscribed in "Torah and the Gospel" (which are) with them. He will enjoin on them that which is right and forbid them that which is wrong. He will make lawful for them all the good things and prohibit for them only the foul, and he will relieve them of their burden and the fetters that they used to wear' (_al-A'rāf,_ 7: 157).

The Crusades and, in their wake, the clergy and the missionaries and those European authors who neither had a bent for research nor possessed religious values, were mainly responsible for keeping Europe estranged from and antagonistic to Islam and its Prophet, peace be upon him. They presented the Prophet, peace be upon him, and his message in shockingly hideous colours as a result of which wildly incredible and false sayings have gained currency. The dark halo created round Islam by such sayings, assiduously propagated for generations, prevented Europe from acknowledging Islam and its Prophet, peace be upon him, and appreciating their greatness. Instances of this vilification can be easily picked out from any book written on them or related subjects during the Middle Ages or even long afterwards. Even today many a zealous Western author refers to and repeats these accusations, though with novel techniques and from new angles.

There has been yet another important reason for Europe's

antagonism, her deliberate hostility towards Islam — that is the presence in Europe of the Turks. The Ottomans were regarded as the sole representatives of Islam and, given that they occupied large portions of Europe and did, sometimes, act violently and unjustly, an objective appraisal of Islam was difficult to achieve.

The consequence of Europe's estrangement from Islam has been profound. Had any European nation accepted its message, world history might have taken a quite different course — civilisation would surely not be rushing insanely towards its own destruction, nor would religion and morality have become so irrelevant and ineffective and life so meaningless — and the East would not have been, as it is, certainly, the easy target for extermination, exploitation and oppression.

NEED OF THE HOUR

The world is suffering from a void, a great lack — it has done for centuries. There is need of a nation that is strong in all respects — a nation that, through believing and propagating the true, final Message, will tackle all the problems of the world and lead humanity to its rightful destiny. Such a nation must unite faith and morality and action — combine modern culture, creativeness, energy, with a will to steer the world from evil towards virtue, from destructiveness towards order and construction.

The Turks under the Ottoman rule, did, in the fifteenth century, perform this role in the East. They led the then Islamic world, giving to it a new life, a new impulse and energy. Partly because of their backwardness in the modern sciences and in organisation, but also because they were continually occupied in repelling European invasions, the Turks could not fulfil the same role in Europe. From the time of the Renaissance which gave birth to a new order, the Turks were outstripped by other nations in Europe. Thus the void remains to be filled by some nation — oriental or occidental — which can combine faith and science, integrate the eternal heavenly message with reason, knowledge and progressive outlook, adapt modern resources to moral objectives, give to a despondent world staring at its own death, hope and meaning, a new future. Only such a nation can be the true leader of mankind; it alone can change the course of history.

This would require a revolution indeed — one to make all others heretofore pale and insignificant by comparison. It would require a tremendous moral and intellectual courage; a tremendous capacity for sacrifice, to move from one way of life to another, from the present order of things to a quite new order, from one faith to another. Such a move would bring to you, the people of Germany, leadership and greatness in the world, and, more importantly — and this was not dreamt of by these bold war-loving leaders who plunged this nation into the horror of two world wars — it would bring respect, a deep peace, a spiritual contentment and joy. A profound revolution of this kind with such an objective — that truly would give right direction to your material power and political supremacy; you would be leaders by being the examples for humanity. Such leadership is promised in the Holy Qur'ān in these verses:

> And We wished to be Gracious to those who were being depressed in the land, to make them leaders (in faith) and make them heirs. (*al-Qaṣaṣ,* 28: 5)

> And We appointed from among them leaders, giving Guidance under Our Command, so long as they persevered with patience and continued to have faith in Our signs. (*al-Sajda,* 32: 24)

Chapter Four

Material Abundance without Faith in God

From Germany Nadwi turns to America.
America today is looked to as the leader of the Western civilisation. It may also be called, rightly, the paradise of material abundance on this planet. But its predicament, according to Nadwi, lies in making a god of man himself — a denial that the will of the Creator rules supreme. Nothing portrays the American predicament, indeed that of the modern age, better than the parable of the man provided with gardens bearing plenteous fruits, in seemingly complete security. If America is friendless today, it is for no reason other than that it is godless.

Muslims who have come to reside in America, says Nadwi, owe a duty to their new abode. To America they must communicate the message of faith in One God. [Ed.]

4

WHAT IS MISSING?

Brothers and sisters, it makes me very happy to be with you here in Washington, the capital city of the United States of America, which may be described as the hub of the world. Today its influence is felt everywhere, and in all spheres of life, social, political and economic. We may like it or not, but no-one can deny it.

How did America acquire this position of pre-eminence? How much does it owe to skill, industry and organisation and how much is on account of our deficiencies? Those are complex questions that we need not go into here.

From the point of view of material progress, this country is a paradise on earth, and, excuse me for saying so, this is what has brought you to it from your native lands, India, Pakistan, Syria, Egypt, Saudi Arabia, and so on. There is no harm in it either, for don't pieces of iron collect around the magnet or thirsty people rush to the place where there is water? I have seen America from coast to coast, both as an ordinary tourist and a student of the Qur'ān and history, and have found something wanting here. And that is exactly what has been alluded to in the Qur'ānic verses we have just heard.

May God bless the learned friend who recited the verses from *Sūra al-Kahf* (18) and reward him generously in both the worlds. He has brought home to us a world of truths and realities, and, by the by, done me a great service. I was thinking what I was going to say at this meeting. There are, of course, so many things one can talk about, and it is difficult to choose. I was wondering what message I should or could offer to you, here in the States, I was wondering what you'd

---

From a speech delivered at the Islamic Centre of Washington on 25 June, 1977, attended, among others, by Indian, Pakistani and Arab scholars. The proceedings began with the recitation by an Egyptian scholar of the passage, 'Set forth to them the parable of two men; for one of them We provided two gardens of grape-vines. . .' from Sūra al-Kahf *(18) which served very appropriately as the theme of the speech.*

like to hear from me, when, suddenly, the Qur'ān rescued me as it always does, and I felt that a wonderful *portrait* of the modern age, which has come to the extreme pinnacle of material development, had been drawn in these verses.

> For one of them We provided two gardens of grape-vines. And surrounded them with date palms; in between the two we placed corn-fields. Both the gardens have their fruit and withheld naught thereof. And We caused a river to gush forth therein. And he had fruit. And he said to his comrade, when he spoke with him: I am more than thee in wealth and stronger in respect of men. (*al-Kahf,* 18: 32-34)

Can a better portrait be drawn of modern America? Gardens of grape-vines! Does not this great land present a spectacle of luxuriance and plentitude? What is lacking in it? What fruit is not found here? All the gifts of the Lord are abundantly available.

And yet there is something sadly wanting to which attention has been drawn by the thoughtful and believing friend in these words:

> When thou entered the garden, why did thou not say: That which Allah willeth (will come to pass)! There is no strength save in Allah! (*al-Kahf,* 18: 39)

That *Māshā' Allāh, lā quwwata illā billāh* (that which Allah willeth; there is no power but in God), that is missing. This *Māshā' Allāh, lā quwwata illā billāh* has the power to turn dust into gold, raise material progress to the level of worship of the highest order, check the rebellious beast of the carnal self so that it becomes a most happy and blessed means for carrying man to his ultimate destination. It is the master key that can open any lock. One thing the Western world does not possess is this. On the face of it, these are just a couple of words which we utter routinely in everyday life. *Māshā' Allāh;* when did you come?' *Māshā' Allāh,* when did you have this new suit made?' And so on. In fact, of course, the expression contains an ocean of profound meaning — only we tend to forget that meaning.

THE WILL OF GOD

Māshā' Allāh has a marvellous power to subdue the materialistic conceptions and conceit of man that lead him into the delusion that whatever is happening around him is of his own choice and making. We utter it mechanically, without the faintest idea of its intrinsic significance, but what *Māshā' Allāh* denotes, in sum, is that whatever takes place in the world is by the command of God and by His power and authority; the credit for it does not go to man, nor does praise belong to him.

> Praise be to Allah, Lord of the Worlds. (*al-Fātiḥa*, 1: 1)

> Allah is He who raised the heavens without any pillars. (*al-Ra'd*, 13: 2)

> But His command, when He intendeth a thing, is only that He saith unto it: Be! and it is. (*Yā Sīn*, 36: 82).

This attribute of the Divine, expressed in such verses as I have quoted, has been compressed into the single pithy phrase — *Māshā' Allāh, lā quwwata illā billāh:* only that which Allah willeth will happen. He is the Author of all things, the Creator of all things. There is no power save in Allah.

Today, America is a living example of 'He hath loaded you with His favours both without and within' (*Luqmān*, 31: 20) and 'Abundantly supplied with sustenance from every place' (*al-Naḥl*, 16: 112). Wealth is here pouring up from the earth and down from the heavens. Then, why is America not a living example to the world of real peace and contentment, of good understanding and security?

WHY AMERICA IS FRIENDLESS

True, the United States can claim to be the benefactor of the world and, God knows, for many people it is the great provider of the daily bread. But how many countries feel sincerely grateful to it? America is giving food, money and arms to scores of nations and aiding them in the implementation of their development plans. But what is it getting in return? A number of countries feel protected against external aggression because of their defence pacts and

68

other arrangements with America. For them its friendship is the greatest guarantee of peace and the preservation of their sovereignty. Yet, no one is giving thanks to it. On the contrary, they never miss an opportunity to denounce it. An undercurrent of hatred is found everywhere against it. America has no sincere friend, no true well-wisher in any part of the world.

Do the leaders of this great country not feel it? Are its thinkers blissfully unaware of this reality? No, they must know that for all its dollars what America is getting back is a kick here and a let-down there. But have they ever tried to go to the root of the matter? A little honest self-study will show that at the bottom of it all lies America's own insincerity. Its entire aid concept and aid machinery is devoid of true magnanimity. Its generosity is a cloak for the exploitation of the weaker and the poorer nations. It gives, not to enable them to stand on their feet, but rather to perpetuate their dependence.

On the other hand, the Prophets devoted their time and energy to the service of mankind and gave it the priceless gifts of faith, truth, sincerity and universal brotherhood, and, as a consequence, nations and communities became their slaves. The Egyptians, Syrians and Iraqis renounced their languages, cultures and ancient civilisations, and willingly accepted the rule of the Arabs, or, rather, of the Muslim Arabs, and even their language. At present, a campaign is being conducted in our Eastern countries against the English language, even to the extent of removing it from the sign-boards: however, so far, not a voice has been raised against the Arabic language in the Arab world. In fact, no reaction or hostility against Islamic civilisation or the Arab-Islamic culture is felt in the Arabic-speaking countries while, perhaps, a feeling of disgust and intolerance is building up against the European civilisation in various parts of the world and the day is not far off when they will throw it out and revive the Eastern or their own indigenous civilisations.

WITHOUT DIVINE LIGHT

There is everything in America save the light of the Book of God and Divine guidance. The belief that it is God who

69

finally directs the affairs of the world, that God has power over all things, and that all that we have achieved is by God's grace and that we should spend what we possess according to His Will and Command, and in His path: this is the one great void in this mighty land.

It has gardens of grape-vines, but not *Māshā' Allāh lā quwwata illā billāh.* In the parable of the two men the possessor of the gardens is a plain materialist, the soul of rebellious ingratitude, an egotist, while the other is a truthful Believer: he is weak, he does not possess gardens of grape-vines, but he is a Believer and God has blessed him with faith. The gardens withhold nothing. They pour out all that they have, like a spring gushing out of the earth, abundantly.

The man says to his richer neighbour, 'Very well, but why did you not say: That which Allah willeth will come to pass; there is no power save in Allah, when you went into the garden? You should have avowed that it all was by the grace and benevolence of the Lord, and a manifestation of His might and mercifulness'.

THE MUSLIM RESPONSIBILITY

America does not say, Americans do not feel, that their wealth and power are the gifts of God. But Why? It is a long and distressing story; shameful, too, for us Muslims. Distressing, because had America been blessed with faith, the history of mankind would have been different and we would have been free from the fear of a nuclear holocaust. Shameful, because it is we Muslims who failed to bring Islam here, despite many opportunities which the Lord gave us. Muslims came to the West when it was beginning its rise, and there was the opportunity during the Muslim rule of Spain to communicate vigorously to the European people the message of Islam. Alas, we Muslims were asleep or too busy building wonderful places and mosques, like al-Hambra and al-Zahra. Our contribution to the distressful circumstance that the world's most powerful nation faces should only shame us. However, even now, for its own sake as well as for the peace of the world, what America urgently needs is to forge a living unity between its own enormous energies and the wisdom of Prophethood. But Christianity can hardly do that.

It has long been and is now ineffective: it has leaned too hard towards monasticism and renunciation of earthly life; it has been (through the Church) too vigorously anti-scientific to be of any use to a modern soul. It attempted to push back the rising tide of knowledge, instead of demonstrating toleration and moderation to the eager, enterprising people of Europe and America. It could not say, like Islam, 'show us the straight path'; or 'Our Lord, give us good in this world, and good in the Hereafter'.

Christianity lost its soul centuries ago when it stepped out of Palestine and entered into the Hellenic-Roman world. Christianity of today is not the Christianity of Jesus; it is the invention of St. Paul (as Neitzsche put it). It cannot guide a dynamic country like America.

It is up to us now to present a forceful and true account of Islam as what it is, a balanced, comprehensive and comprehensible picture of how man and God must relate.

SUBMIT TO GOD

To the citizens of the United States we say: our best wishes to you. We do not grudge you your attainments. We don't regard your progress with contempt. What we do ask you most earnestly is only to add *Māshā' Allāh, wa lā quwwata illā billāh* to what you have. Subordinate your worldly possessions and phenomenal achievements to the will of God. Place it all under the control and authority of the Divine law. Use it for the rebirth and rescue of mankind; for the generation of an atmosphere of universal (non-exclusive) equality and fraternity and justice, and freedom from fear in the world. Let there be no distinctions of race, colour or wealth between man and man. Use your enormous resources for the reconstruction of the world's economies. You will in this way be helping yourselves as well, for your civilisation cannot otherwise survive for long. Iqbal put it well:

> The arrant intellect that laid bare the treasures of nature,
> In its own nest is threatened by the lightning it has released.

Muslims do not renounce the world but regard it as an important transitional stage in man's onward journey, for his real and final home is in the Hereafter. Their attitude towards

71

life is governed by the Qur'ānic verse which says:

> And for that Abode of the Hereafter We assign it unto those who seek not oppression in the earth, nor yet corruption. The (good) sequel is for those who ward off (evil). (*al-Qaṣaṣ*, 28: 83)

To conclude, let me thank you for coming here to give a Muslim brother a patient hearing. May Allah protect you and your faith, and may your next generation also be believers in Islam.

> Do not die save as Muslims. (*al-Baqara*, 2: 132)

My fervent prayer is that you remain true to this commandment. May you bow your heads low before God, perform Prayers regularly and adhere steadfastly to the *kalima* as long as you live in this world, and when you depart from it, may the radiance of faith be in your hearts and the *kalima* of *lā ilāha illallāh, Muḥammadur Rasūlullāh* on your lips!

Chapter Five

Slavery to Machines

The bliss of material abundance that the American paradise offers has been brought about as a result of tremendous progress that she has made in science and technology. Yet technology is not a neutral force which only serves man; it tries to become his master. If man is without faith in God, points out Nadwi, he is quite likely to become a slave to his machines. America, as it is today, is a living testimony to this truth.

Submission to one God — Islam — raises a man to the level of the vicegerency of God; it gives him freedom from servility to many gods. America, despite its mastery over the world, has itself become a slave to its own creations because it has forsaken the true God. Unfortunately Christianity did not have the capability to protect America from falling into this abyss. [Ed.]

5

I am here, as you know, at the invitation of the Muslim Community Centre; I acknowledge with deep gratitude the opportunity not only of coming to this great land but also of seeing it from coast to coast, of meeting people and speaking to them. It is indeed a new world for me — not, of course, in the sense that it was for Columbus, but new from the viewpoint of a student who possesses some knowledge of religion. I have travelled from New York to California and also visited Canada, covering in these few weeks some 4,000 miles. I address you, now, at the end of the tour. Naturally you will be curious to know my impressions. Coming as I do from a country that is, so to speak, backward in relation to the developments in the West, I should have remarked with enthusiasm upon the phenomenal developments in evidence here — but you are more familiar with them than I, and it is therefore unnecessary. So, let me begin with the following verses of Jalāluddīn Rūmī, verses Allama Iqbal uses to open *Asrār-i-Khūdī*, 'Secrets of the Self', his long Persian poem:

> Last night the Shaikh wandered about the town with a lamp.
> Saying: 'I am tired of demon and beast; man is my desire.
> My heart is sick of the feeble-hearted fellow-traveller;
> The Lion of God and Rustam-i-Dāstān are my desire.
> I said, 'We too searched for him, but he couldn't be found'.
> He replied 'what cannot be found — that thing is my desire'.

Rūmī tells of a sage wandering the dark town streets, lamp in hand, as though in search of some long-lost thing. The poet wants to know what that thing is, and the sage explains that he is tired of 'demon and beast', tired of living where the 'feeble-spirited' live like animals, and in this sickness he desires the Lion of God Haḍrat 'Alī, or Rustam the son of Zal, the great hero of pre-Islamic Persia, to restore his faith in man. And, when the poet responds that this is an

---

From a speech delivered at the Muslim Community Centre, Chicago, on 19 June, 1977, before a large gathering of educated Muslims.

impossible quest, the wise old man tells him that even so, it is the rare and unattainable that he seeks.

Perhaps what Rūmī says will surprise you, for he lived in Anatolia, not a backward place — on the contrary, it was one of the most advanced regions of the then civilised world, where the foundations of the magnificent Seljuk kingdom were about to be laid. He was born in Balkh in Iran, the most civilised country of those days, that could justly be described as the Greece of the East — in philosophy and literature its glorious contribution has left an indelible mark on the pages of history. Nevertheless, Rūmī was sick at heart and in those verses he tries to show the wounds deep inside his heart. He tells the story through the 'wise man' but it is his own story: he pines for man; even in that wonderful city, that land of culture and enlightenment, he pines for man. There is everything to be found there — stately mansions, flourishing gardens, exotic food, elegance of dress and manners — but not man. To be sure, there are human forms and figures, but not real men. Rūmī's thought is more explicit in another verse where he says:

> These are not men, only men's faces they have,
> Slaves of the stomach, victims of sensuality.

MEN OR SLAVES TO MACHINES?

I have seen of America what could be seen during a brief stay, travelling from north to south, east to west. What has struck me most is the supremacy of machines. The flowering here is the flowering of commerce and technology: the physical sciences have reached the utmost point of their development and given whatever they could by way of progressively greater ease and luxury.

But how would you answer if asked how many real men lived in this country, humming as it is with vigorous activity? Men whose hearts beat and eyes moisten for the sake of humanity? Men who hold the reins of life and carnal desire instead of being driven by them? Men who are aware of their Creator and whose hearts are filled with love for Him and respect for mankind? Who lead a simple life, in harmony with nature, and are conscious of true joy and genuine contentment? Who do not thrill to tension and conflict in the world, who hate rather the greed and selfishness of the politicians? Men who wish every country well and wish it prosperity, eager rather to give than grab? Who do not believe the aim of life to be eating, drinking and being merry, but discover the greater happiness of feeding another man and going hungry themselves? Men who dream of the reconstruction of the world and are not solely preoccupied with the growth and power of their own land? Who really want to see the world united — not on the transitory and artificial platform of the United Nations but on the real and natural basis of the oneness of mankind? Men who know the beginning and end of existence and remain mindful of it; who understand that they would not, after completing their span of life, merely perish in dust like insects, but would have to go somewhere and render account of how they used the tremendous capabilities with which God endowed them? And what capabilities — to impart energy to stones, to conquer the air and the oceans, to harness the rays of the sun, even to walk on the moon. Men who feel that their glory does not lie in breathing life into inanimate matter and subjugating the world through it, but in bringing life to themselves.

God created man and created him vicegerent of the world and all its resources, of all matter, not to be the slave of matter but to make matter his slave or, rather, to make it God's slave, to employ it in the fulfilment of God's will.

I ask again, how many real men live in this country, capable of the vicegerency of the world in the way God meant it? How many who do not see greatness in subjugating other peoples, but see it instead in the selfless service of mankind, in putting an end to the exploitation of one country or community by another? How many in America aspire to release humanity from slavery to the inordinate acquisitiveness of power, wealth, even intellect?

ONE BOND, UNLIMITED FREEDOM

Islam raised the head of the bedouin Arab so high that he could say to Rustam, Commander-in-Chief of Persia, and say very plainly — 'We have been sent by Allah to deliver whom He wills from the overlordship of His slaves, of men like him, to His own overlordship; from the narrowness of the world to its boundlessness, from the oppressiveness of other religions to the justice of Islam'. And he could say this, the poor bedouin, to the mighty Rustam whose very name was enough to strike terror into an enemy's heart — 'God has appointed us to rescue men from the worship of fellow men and lead them to the worship of no one save God; to bring men out of the prison you so grandly name the Persian Empire into the wide, limitless world of God, into the open air of freedom. We pity not ourselves but you. It is your wretchedness that has evoked sympathy in our hearts and drawn us so far from the desert land of Arabia. We come to set you free from the golden cage in which you are as captive as the nightingales are in theirs, and bring you to the boundless kingdom of God. You are the slaves of your desires and habits, of your musicians and cooks and water-bearers, while we are the slaves of God. We come to deliver you from the innumerable forms of slavery into the one and only true freedom — that in God'.

Truly, freedom is one; servility and slavery manyfold. For the darkness has many faces, but light is one. Thus, *nūr* (light) is always singular in the Qur'ān as, for instance, in the passage: 'Allah is the protecting friend of those who believe. He brings them out of *ẓulumāt* into *nūr*' (*al-Baqara*, 2: 257). (*'Ẓulumāt'* is the plural of *'ẓulmat'*, meaning darkness). Why is *nūr* always singular? Not because the Arabic language has no plural for it, but because light is one, its origin is one — the awareness of God. There is no other source of guidance if the light from God is not available. Reflecting upon America, the following verses of Iqbal come to mind:

> Though Europe is radiant with the light of knowledge,
> The 'Ocean of Darkness' is barren of the 'Fount of Life'.

> A nation unblessed by Divine light,
> Steam and electricity bound its works.

Iqbal never visited the United States, but his knowledge of the West is deeper than ours. There is an old saying that the 'Fountain of Life' is found in the 'Ocean of Darkness'. Alexander, reportedly, made Khawaja Khiḍr (said to be a

Prophet who discovered the 'Fountain of Life' and drank of it) his guide and requested him to conduct him to the waters of immortality in the 'Ocean of Darkness' — but even Khawaja Khiḍr confessed inability. Iqbal observes, alluding to this, that the West is like an Ocean of Darkness lacking the Fountain of Life. The West made the material world its focus and limit of endeavour, and progress within it the highest goal of that endeavour. Of course the West has been staggeringly successful; because it is the way of God that He makes His help available, in fullest measure, to man, in whatever sphere man chooses for his attention. The heart of the problem is making the right choice. What, then, is the final outcome for a people, deprived of the light of Divine guidance, who turn their back upon Prophets, who rely wholly upon human reason, devoting all their energies to matter, to mass manufacture and to weapons; who conquer matter, but not the soul, who subjugate the world, but not the spirit?

THE ROLE OF CHRISTIANITY

Those of you who have studied the history of Western civilisation and read J. W. Draper's *History of the Conflict between Religion and Science* will agree that once Europe was converted to Christianity there could be no outcome but a headlong plunge into materialism. Christianity offered no encouragement to intellect, nor gave a practical guidance for the organisation of society. It wanted to take Europe backwards while the Europeans, eager and restless by temperament, wanted to press onward. Opportunity and achievement lay before them and the competition for advancement urged them to stop at nothing. They could not rest content with a narrow sphere of growth and progress in which they had to live by the Bible and ask the clerics whether such-and-such a thing was or was not lawful. It was a tragedy not only for Europe but for the whole world that Christianity fell to its lot. No religion was more inimical to the spirit of Europe and the natural disposition of its people, just as, as a little thought will show, no religion was more in keeping with its genius and capable of giving it a proper sense of direction than Islam.

According to Christian doctrine man is born with the heavy load of original sin on his head. How then can he have faith in himself? How can a man who is feeling ashamed, because he is born a sinner, look boldly at the universe, discover the forces of nature, plumb the depths of the oceans and dream of reaching the planets? How can a man who believes that sin is ingrained in his nature, that he is in need of an external atonement to be offered on his behalf, undertake with bold pride the discovery and conquest of nature? Here was a contradiction the parallel of which can scarcely be found in the world. It was as if two horses had been harnessed to opposite ends of the cart. Under the influence of climatic and other environmental factors, the Europeans were eager to go forward, to do something, but Christianity pulled them back towards monasticism. The clerics openly preached that earthly life was a bad business, and that the spiritual advancement of man lay in escape from it. Ideally, to attain salvation, a man should live in the mountains, dedicate his life to the Church, and practise celibacy. A perusal of Lecky's *History of European Morals* will reinforce the point. Such was the Christianity that reached the West. In the event the West decided that if it was to progress, it should not only free itself from the shackles of the Church, but also take leave of all religion. Significantly enough, while the decline of the Muslim world started when it abandoned Islam, the rise of the West began when it forsook Christianity.

SLAVERY TO MACHINES

The culmination of that process has, today, made America a slave of machines. The supremacy of the United States is accepted all over the world and its hand is seen in everything that happens anywhere. No country, Muslim or non-Muslim, is altogether free from its control or influence, felt in one form or another. Plans are made here and enforced in our countries, and our own leaders implement them. Today, America has enslaved the world, but it has, itself, become the slave of its technologies. It is a prisoner of its way of life, of material progress, of factories and laboratories, of fancy goods and gadgets. One thing that I did not see here was 'man', a real man whose heart was alive and awake, and not the working part of a machine. Man, here, has become so thoroughly adapted to technology and an artificial environment, that his ideas and emotions too have become mechanical. The properties of rock and iron have entered into his soul. He has become narrow, selfish, cold, unfeeling, impervious to the needs of humanity. There is no warmth in his heart; no moisture in his eyes. This is the unhappy reality that I have observed during my stay in America.

Chapter Six

Had America been Blessed
with Islam!

Nadwi starts by acknowledging, ungrudgingly, the great progress that has been made by America, and other Western nations in many areas of human civilisation. This has been possible because all their energies have remained concentrated on material progress. They have failed to pay attention to the immense world of 'heart' that lies within. Had they received the Divine guidance, their own fate and the fate of the entire world would have been different; history would have taken a new course.

For this unfortunate situation, apart from Christianity, Muslims are to blame and 'no amount of regret is too much'. Islam, in every respect, is the more suitable religion for mankind. It is free of doctrines like original sin, incarnation and atonement. Unfortunately, as Europe turned back from Christianity it turned back from religion and worship also.

Muslims, now living in America, must come forward and shoulder the heavy responsibility for making amends for past shortcomings. They should not be engrossed in merely acquiring higher education or earning money.

True there is no Muslim society which can serve as an example of Islam. But there is no reason to despair. Did not the Prophet, peace be upon him, without much power or strength, extend an invitation to the mightiest emperors of his time to come and submit to One God? Shall those Muslims who have chosen to live in America fail to follow his example? [Ed.]

6

Surely We created man of the best stature
Then We reduced him to the lowest of the low.

(*al-Tīn*, 95: 4-5)

Friends and brothers — I begin, as these verses of the Qur'ān suggest to me, with a statement that may well startle you: the Western world, right across from Europe to the Americas, is most fortunate, and yet it is most unfortunate. Such a contradiction in one and the same breath may seem strange to you. But the verses just read to you — they too appear self-contradictory, though they convey a profound reality. What is true of man is also true of this part of the world. Like the whole of the West, America is at once lucky and unlucky, and this state of affairs is of serious concern because, for reasons I have discussed at length in my book, *Islam and the West,* this country has been vested by God with leadership of the world. Nations have risen to great heights in the past and then declined into obscurity, but no nation ever before has exercised such worldwide influence, owned such power and prestige — for this reason America's situation affects the whole world, and we must all take note.

THE LAND OF PLENTY
America is fortunate because nature has been most generous to it. The Lord has bestowed His gifts lavishly upon this country. Its people are resourceful and enterprising, full of enthusiasm for living. They have been granted such tenacity of purpose, such resolution, that they have made their country a paradise. They have unravelled nature's mysteries and harnessed its forces to their use. In the words

---

From a speech delivered on 6 June, 1977, in the Hall of the Divinity College of Harvard University. The audience included University teachers and scholars with a large number of students from different parts of the country also attending. The occasion began with the recital of Sūra al-Tīn *by a black American Muslim.*

of Iqbal, they have 'enchained the rays of the sun', and 'sought the orbits of the stars'. America has become like a land where wealth pours down like rain and rivers of milk and honey flow. This is the result of the pragmatism, robust imagination and unflagging eagerness of the American people. There are here not only mineral resources, but also the hands and will to exploit them. In this respect, America is exceedingly fortunate and the whole world is, as it were, keenly conducting itself as if to prove it. Everyone is a beggar at America's door, eager to solicit its favours, keenly desirous of acknowledging the ingenuity, sense of discipline, the management skills of its people, who have organised their life so well that the world at large is benefiting from it in some measure.

Be envious of America, admire it: I do not believe in partisanship whether religious, social or political — one should give praise where praise is due. But, at the same time, this country is, I must insist, most unfortunate. I say it with a full sense of responsibility. Many of you may be shocked, but it is a fact.

THE LAND OF MISFORTUNE

It has been a tragedy, not only for America but the whole of mankind, that its people have concentrated exclusively on material progress, making the physical world the sole sphere of their activity. It would have been a different story had they received correct guidance and the blessing of true faith, had they been attentive to morality with equal earnestness and enthusiasm, and looked for the signs of God in *anfus,* within themselves, and not only in *āfāq,* the horizons. If the intellectual faculties of the Americans had been directed also towards the discovery of the secrets of the self — of heart and soul — they would have realised that the world of heart and soul is immeasureably more extensive than the world of matter, so much so that if the whole of the universe was dropped into the heart of man it would be lost like a pebble in an ocean. The people of America would, then, have been able to appreciate, to assess more wisely and correctly, the place of man in the grand design of creation. Of the time and energy they have recklessly spent on material sciences — with what results we all know — we have in the Qur'ān:

> And that man hath only that for which he maketh effort,
> And that his effort will be seen,
> And afterward he will be repaid for it with fullest payment. (*al-Najm,* 53: 39-41)

> Each do We supply, both these and those, from the bounty of thy Lord;
> And the bounty of the Lord can never be walled up. (*al-Isrā',* 17: 20)

Whatever field man chooses for himself, God will grant him success in it. There is no limit: thus far and no further. The consequences of the enterprise and industry of the West are before us. The world has shrunk and man has subjugated it to his own ends and interests. Had the Westerners exerted themselves, in the same way, on the heart, soul, and faith, the world would have known the true station of humanity. When the West applied its arts to a tree, it produced a fruit no one could dream of. Likewise when it turned to physics, chemistry and botany, it discovered new worlds. In earlier times people doubted the plurality of the worlds and those who made such a claim were remorselessly punished by the Papal authority. But today, a new world is being discovered in almost everything. So, we may wonder, had the West known the true station of humanity and appreciated the distinction God has conferred upon man, what new world would have been discovered, what different course history would have taken.

Two events were largely responsible for the tragedy which has overtaken not only the West but the whole of mankind. One was the advent and success of Christianity in the Western hemisphere. For the other, we Muslims are also to blame and no amount of regret is too much.

GULF BETWEEN ISLAM AND THE WEST

The fact is that the most appropriate religion for this part of the world would have been Islam which awakens man's latent capabilities, encourages his intellect, and makes him self-reliant and self-respecting. Says the Qur'ān:

Surely We created man of the best stature. (*al-Tīn*, 95: 4)

Verily We have honoured the children of Adam. We carry them on the land and the sea, and have made provision of good things for them, and have preferred them over many of those whom We created with a marked preferment. (*al-Isrā'*, 17: 70)

Lo! I am about to place a viceroy in the earth. (*al-Baqara*, 2: 30)

Islam places the crown of vicegerency on man's head; there can be no greater honour. The whole structure of Islam is based upon the doctrine of Divine Unity, and when it declares that man is *Khalīfatullāh,* the vicegerent of God on earth, it elevates him so much that one cannot think of a higher and nobler concept of humanity. Thus, in a Tradition, it is stated that on the Day of Judgement God will say to His servants, 'I fell ill and you did not visit Me'. The servant will reply, 'Thou art the Lord of the Worlds. How could I visit Thee?' God will, thereupon, say, 'Did you not know that such-and-such a servant of Mine was ill and you did not care to visit him? Had you gone to see him in order to comfort or help, you would have found Me with him'. God, again, will say, 'O son of Adam! I asked you for food, but you did not give it to Me'. The servant will reply, 'Thou art the Lord of the Worlds. How could I give Thee food?' God will then say, 'Are you not aware that such-and-such a servant of Mine begged you for food and you did not give it to him. Had you fed him you would have found him with Me'. God, again, will say, 'O son of Adam! I was naked, but you did not cover Me with a garment'. The servant will reply, 'Thou art the Lord of the Worlds. How could I clothe Thee?' God will then say, 'Such-and-such a servant of Mine begged you for something to wear and you did not give it to him. Had you done so the garment would have reached Me'.

What greater honour can there be for mankind? Islam, further, teaches that man is sinless and pure by nature. A Tradition has it that 'every child is born "of its nature", i.e. pure and guiltless, and it is its parents who make it a Jew, Christian or Fire-worshipper'. They dye it in their own colour, otherwise the newborn is 'of the colour of Allah'.

Islam teaches that the fundamental reality of human nature is submission. There is no defect in it. It is basically sound.

The Qur'ān says: 'It gets what it earns, and it suffers what it earns' (*al-Baqara*, 2: 286). This means that what man earns in harmony with nature is beneficial for him, and what he earns by wilful defiance is harmful for him: the good a man does is in conformity with his nature while the wrong he pursues is in defiance of it. This view that the good deeds of man correspond to his nature whereas his misdeeds are, so to speak, a revolt against himself, argues powerfully for the inherent purity and innocence of human nature. If a man falls into error it is a passing phase, and when he offers sincere repentance, the consequence of that error for the man passes away, the rust on his heart disappears. Repentance is natural, not contrived, and a high place is given in Islam to those who repent after sinning.

Islam is the most suitable religion for this land. Had a union taken place between the two, the history of mankind would have taken a very different course. On the one side, the unbounded natural resources of America, the tremendous vitality, resoluteness and enterprise of its people; on the other, the moderation of Islam, its message of hope and confidence, its unequalled distinctiveness as the faith of nature, its insistence on the intrinsic innocence of man.

Islam strongly encourages creativeness in man and arouses his dormant capabilities. There is no over-nice speculative philosophy nor impossible empty idealism in it. It is based upon a robust sense of the realities of life, and is such a simple religion that anyone with an open heart can easily understand it. It does not put fetters on the mind, nor place obstacles in the path of knowledge, but elevates learning to an act of worship. It calls on man to study and reflect, to make fullest use of his intelligence.

> And in earth are signs (*āyāt*) for those whose faith is sure, and (also) in yourselves. Can ye then not see? (*al-Dhāriyāt*, 51: 20-21)

> (Who) reflect upon the creation of the heavens and the earth (and say): Our Lord. Thou createdst not this in vain. (*Āl 'Imrān*, 3: 191)

We shall show them Our signs on the horizons and within themselves. (*Fuṣṣilat,* 41: 53)

And those who, when they are reminded of the revelations of their Lord, fall not deaf and blind thereat (but listen attentively and cogitate). (*al-Furqān,* 25: 73)

THE WEST AND CHRISTIANITY
But, Islam is not the faith in America, a misfortune for this country and for the world. The Western world opted for a religion which insisted on the doctrine of original sin, giving rise to the worst pessimism and leading man to believe that sin was his destiny. It did not raise the stature of man, but put the mark of disgrace on his forehead, persuading him to believe that he needed an 'other' to redeem him by offering atonement for his misdeeds. To make matters worse, the tendency to monasticism and renunciation quickly established itself in the West and deepened further the ill-effects of the doctrine of original sin.

Equally calamitous was the attitude of the Church, when in power, to new knowledge. The clerics blocked the path of investigation. At a time when Europe was waking up and breaking its intellectual chains, Papal authority stood before it like a brick wall and started measuring everything with its own yardstick. The Church opposed when it was claimed that the earth was round. Bruno, whose only crime was that he taught the plurality of worlds, was declared a heretic and burnt alive, and Galileo another scientist of no less worth, was imprisoned for life for believing that the earth moved round the sun. The Inquisition, established to tackle heresy, performed its duty with such alacrity that the number of persons tried and punished by it was, in no way, less than the casualties in the last war.

THE CHOICE OF MATERIALISM
Inevitably, Europe turned and turned decidedly towards materialism. The enlightened sections among the Europeans developed a strong aversion to everything associated with the clerics, a definite intolerance of every kind of spiritual control. Their feelings of disgust and disdain were directed

not against a particular religion, but against the whole concept of religious belief and worship. In its haste, the West decided that no progress could be made until religion was discouraged and bondage to the Church ended. Europe thus rose openly in revolt against the Church and set out on the journey of materialism, the mournful consequences of which everywhere stare us in the face.

It is a long and painful story. You are all aware of it. I will, therefore, not go into details.

No one knows the mysteries of the universe save God, nor can anyone say, positively, what lies in store for us tomorrow. But, as the case is at present, this civilisation has reached the highest point of its development, it has brought forth the best fruits it was capable of bearing. Now, we are standing at the crossroads. Western civilisation has almost completed its task and can proudly claim to have lifted almost every veil from the face of nature and unfolded almost all its secrets — distances have shrunk and man is enjoying all the facilities and material benefits he could think of.

Nevertheless, the heart of man is devoid of peace. His soul is unhappy. He has reached a stage where life seems less than meaningless, even pointless. He is dazed and bewildered. What is needed at this juncture is people born in this very country who can pull it out of the morass of frustration and disillusionment, give it a new message and breathe new life into it. Life has been moving at a pace that has left man breathless. Modern civilisation is taking him at break-neck speed he knows not where — nor are the reins in his hands.

THE FUTURE BELONGS TO ISLAM

I do not believe in the philosophy of chance happenings. I feel that there is the Hand of God behind everything that takes place. 'That is the Measuring of the Mighty, the Wise' (*Yā Sīn,* 36: 38). It is no accident that you Muslims have come to live here in large numbers. There are manual workers among you and students engaged in valuable and original scientific research. In all walks of life you will make your mark, have some influence. What is more, Islam is spreading in America. It has made a dent. A number of Americans have either embraced Islam or are ready to do so. Our black

Muslim brethren are a source of strength to us. This country, in brief, seems to be taking a new turn and a new ray of hope is appearing. Due to our shortsightedness and internal dissensions, we, in the past, lost the opportunity to come to its aid. Had Islam been propagated in Europe when the Ottomans had established their rule over a part of the Continent, or, even earlier, when the Moors had swept over Spain, the West, today, would not be finding itself in this predicament. It would not have been caught in the quagmire of materialism.

But, unfortunately, we did not rise to the occasion. How I wish that the Muslim evangelists had reached here when they set out into the world in the early centuries of Islam. It is said that the Muslims discovered America before Columbus. How wonderful if they had taken advantage of it and given the message of Islam to the New World. But it was not to be, and the Islamic countries have been paying the penalty for the last two hundred years. I believe that the way the Muslim countries have, today, become the lackeys of the West and the treatment they are receiving at its hands is best thought of as a punishment of their failure to convey to the West the Message of God.

But now the circumstances are taking a favourable turn. Muslims are migrating to America in a steady stream from different lands and for different reasons. There is no Islamic country whose finest young men are not found here. Lastly, a large number of enterprising people are also coming to it from the country where the Ka'ba is situated.

You should, now, realise your responsibility which does not lie merely in acquiring higher education or solving your economic problems. You are not here only to earn and take back the money to your native lands and provide for your families. You should know that it is your duty to give this country what it lacks. If you look at its material attainments and scientific advancement, it presents a true picture of the Divine pronouncement, 'Surely We created man of the best stature', but if you think over its moral decay and the agony of its soul, you will find it at the level of 'the lowest of the low'. The country that claims to have solved all the physical problems is finding itself helpless in providing a solution to

89

the moral crisis of its youth. As Iqbal said:

> He who enchained the sunbeams could not
> Unfurl the dawn on life's dark night.

I say without hesitation that there is no Muslim country which can look the Westerners in the face and say: 'See, it is here that you stumbled. With us is the panacea of your ills and the balm for your inner wounds. It is the Qur'ān and the teachings of our Prophet'. The bitter truth is that we have made ourselves unworthy of speaking to the West like men. We carry a heavy load of gratitude to it on our heads, and are immersed from head to foot in its favours. Our ignorance deposes against us. Our poverty shouts from the house-tops. Our arm is stretched out for alms. Such being the case, how can an Islamic country speak, like an equal, to the West which has the whip hand and enjoys every kind of superiority — intellectual, political, military, economic? Which Muslim country is there that can express the mildest criticism of the West or offer a suggestion?

But the Qur'ān and the example of the Prophet, peace be upon him, fill me with faith and hope. The Blessed Prophet, sent the following epistle to Caesar, who ruled over half of the then known world, when there was not enough to eat in his own house and the Muslim State had not been established in Madina:

> In the Name of Allah, the Most Benevolent, the Most Merciful.
> From Muḥammad, the bondsman and Messenger of Allah, to Heraclius, the Emperor of Rome.
>
> Peace be upon him who follows the Guidance. I invite you to the message of Islam. Accept Islam and you shall be delivered: two-fold will be Allah's reward to you. But if you turn away then on you will rest the sin of (the denial of) your community. O People of the Scripture! Come to an agreement on a thing that is common between us and you: that we shall worship none but Allah, and that we shall ascribe no partner unto Him, and that none of us shall take others for lords beside Allah. And if you turn your back upon it then bear witness that we are they who have surrendered (unto Him).

I am a follower of that Prophet, peace be upon him, who, with utmost trust in God, gave the call of Islam to the mightiest ruler of his time and in circumstances of utter poverty and powerlessness. When the stove had not been lit in his house for months, when members of his household had not had a decent meal even for two consecutive days, when his coffers were empty and his followers few in number, he said to the Roman Emperor, 'Accept Islam and you shall be delivered'.

We are the followers of that Prophet, peace be upon him. We must summon up courage to give to these people what they need; to make them realise that we possess what they are, regrettably, wanting in, and without which Western civilisation is doomed to commit suicide. If anything can save it, it is the guidance of the Qur'ān. A harmonious blending has to be worked out between material progress and spiritual values. Disaster awaits the world if materialism gains the upper hand over morality. This is the call our Islamic countries should give. They should say plainly to the West, 'You are drowning and we can save you'. But is anyone of them in that position? We have forfeited the right to do so. We are the hangers-on of the West. None of the Islamic countries has the courage to speak so to the West. They consider Western civilisation the last word: as someone has said, 'The *Qibla*[1] of the world is *Ḥaram,*[2] and the *Qibla* of *Ḥaram* is America'. I make bold to say that, today, the Islamic countries and the Muslim ruling classes are incapable of giving any call to the West.

But I urge upon you that you do have something to give the Americans. True enough they possess everything, but they are paupers within, bankrupt within.

Fill their bowl with your grain. Display self-confidence, present before them a solid example of the Islamic way of life. Be grateful to God. Through *Ṣalāt,* the sincere Prayer, through freedom from servility to worldly ends and interests, you should demonstrate to the Americans that materialism

---

1. The place to which Muslims turn in prayer.
2. The holy Ka'ba in Makka.

can never enslave you. The Hereafter is an article of faith with you. You hold as true that there is to come another life and another world at the end of this mortal life. You believe that God is All-powerful, He has control over all things, and His good pleasure is the extreme limit of felicity and good fortune. God has given you the opportunity to acquaint the Americans with the realities that have receded into oblivion and that Christianity, despite the vast resources at its disposal, has failed to revive. You can discharge that responsibility, all your faults and weaknesses notwith-standing.

Friends — I have taken a lot of your time. But you must make allowance for the burning of my heart. I can attest before the Lord to have given the *adhān* in the biggest idol-hall of the world, and offered His Guidance. I shall deem myself successful if I have been able to evoke a sympathetic response in even one of my listeners here.

May Allah take from you, in an increasing degree, the service of His faith and make you more useful to Islam and to this country than to yourselves, than even to your families, and to your native lands.

Chapter Seven

Islam: The Most Suitable Religion for Mankind

The role of the Prophet Muhammad, peace be upon him, and the revealed message which he communicated to mankind were revolutionary; they brought about a radical transformation in society. Man was freed from slavery to innumerable nameless and arbitrary forces into the service of One God. He was raised from an abject position to one of supremacy second only to God. He learned of the dignity of man, and the universal brotherhood and equality of all men before God. He was given a new purpose in life, and with the gift of his own free-will became master of his destiny as never before. It is difficult to imagine a more fundamental revolution nor one whose dynamic has continued for so long. The forces which transformed man in the seventh century still have the power to inspire him today. [Ed.]

THE REVOLUTIONARY MESSAGE

The liberal and revolutionary aspects of Islam and its Prophet Muhammad, peace be upon him, which transformed society in the seventh century, are still today amongst the most potent forces at work for the betterment of humanity. They brought not only a new ideology, but inspired the energy and confidence which so radically altered man and the society in which he lived. They provided the impetus for a new age of culture and civilisation, arts and learning, material and spiritual progress.

THE ONENESS OF GOD

What was the nature of the service rendered to mankind? What were the gifts of the Prophet, peace be upon him, that so profoundly affected man and society as he found it? First and foremost he proclaimed belief in the Oneness of God. No more revolutionary, more life-giving and more profitable creed could have been vouchsafed to humanity. Man had been proud and presumptuous, boastful of his creations. He took pride in enslaving other countries and nations, often arrogating to himself even the position of God; yet at the same time he demeaned himself by bowing his head before idols, inanimate, lifeless objects, artifacts of his own creation. He subjected himself to the elemental forces of nature and war, a slave to credulous belief and irrational fears of demons and devils. His life was spent in fear of the unknown and helpless belief in nameless powers, which could not but foster confusion, cowardice, doubt and indecision. By removing the fear of all else save God alone, the Prophet of Islam made him a self-reliant, courageous, rational believing being. It was through Muhammad that man came to recognise his Creator as the Supreme Power, the sole

This chapter, by the author, is taken from The Challenge of Islam, *(ed. Altaf Gauhar, London: Islamic Council of Europe, 1978, pp. 16-30).*

Enricher and Destroyer of life. By submitting only to the will of the one true God, man was freed from servility to other powers. He was enabled to see the unity of Cause in the multiplicity of phenomena; he was reassured of his pivotal position in the scheme of creation; he became aware of his worth and dignity. In short, by accepting the role of servant to the One and only God, he became master of every other created being and object. For the first time man became aware of the exalted position allotted to him by God in the scheme of things.

Unity of Godhead came to be recognised, thanks to the last Prophet, peace be upon him, as the guiding principle for all schools of thought. The power of his message undermined the Polytheistic religions of the day. Pagan belief and practice, though it persisted, suffered a blow from which it never recovered. Man was released from slavery to creation. Could there be a greater gift to humanity than this?

EQUALITY OF MEN

The second great favour conferred by the Messenger of God on human beings was the concept of the equality and brotherhood of all mankind. Before him the world was divided into innumerable castes and creeds, tribes and nations, some claiming nobility for themselves and condemning others to the position of serfs and chattels. It was from Muhammad, peace be upon him, that the world first heard the revolutionary message of human equality:

> O Mankind, Your God is one and you have but one father, You are all progeny of Adam, and Adam was made of clay. Lo! the noblest among you, in the sight of God, is the best in conduct. No Arab has any preference over a non-Arab save by his piety.

The Prophet, peace be upon him, made this declaration on the occasion of his last _Hajj_ before a congregation of one hundred and twenty-four thousand. His announcement put the seal on the twin principles of the Unity of God and the Unity of Mankind. These are the two natural foundations for raising any edifice of peace and progress, friendship and co-operation between different peoples and nations. Together

95

they create a bond of brotherhood between human beings — that of One Lord and One Father for them all. Oneness of God is the spiritual principle of human equality; common lineage of high and low, white and coloured, places all men on the same plane of humanity.

So radical a message was not well received. The world was in no mind to listen to a message which struck so sharply at the roots of existing social relationships and economic and political order. Its cataclysmic consequences threw the world into confusion. This was a time when numerous clans and families claimed their descent from the sun or moon. The Pharaohs of Egypt had believed themselves to be the reincarnation of the sun-god, while in India several ruling families claimed their descent from the sun and moon. The Emperors of Iran called themselves *Kisra* or *Chosroes* implying that Divine blood flowed in their veins. The Chinese rulers too, deemed themselves to be the sons of Heaven. According to the Qur'ān even:

> The Jews and the Christians say that they are the children of God and those whom He loves. (*al-Mā'ida,* 5: 18)

Even amongst the Arabs things were little better. So proud were they of their language that every other nation besides their own was an *'Ajamī* or dumb to them. Further, the Quraish of Makka, being extremely conscious of maintaining their superiority, claimed a position of privilege even in the performance of *Ḥajj.* This was the shape of all things all over the world, when the Qur'ān heralded that all human beings were equal:

> O Mankind! Lo! We have created you male and female, and have made you nations and tribes that ye may know one another. Lo! the noblest of you, in the sight of Allah, is the best in conduct. Lo! Allah is Knower, Aware. (*al-Hujurāt,* 49: 13)

In the opening *Sūra* of the Qur'ān, Allah is invoked as:

> Lord of the Worlds (*al-Fātiḥa,* 1: 1)

96

Man had been accustomed to associate nobility with those who claimed themselves to be the progeny of gods and demi-gods. In order that the honour of the common man was not usurped again by the selected few, the Prophet, peace be upon him, announced:

> The whole of mankind is the family of God and he amongst His family, is dearest to Him, who does good to others.

Today we find the principle of human equality enshrined in the constitutions of different countries and proclaimed from the forum of the United Nations Organisation in the shape of the Charter of Human Rights. Yet long before the days of UN charters, it was in Islam that the concept of equality was first proclaimed as a human right. The indefatigable efforts of Muhammad, peace be upon him, and his followers to create a truly egalitarian Muslim society established the principle later adopted as the basis for human existence throughout the world.

HUMAN DIGNITY

The third great gift bestowed by the Prophet of Islam, peace be upon him, is the concept of human dignity. During the age of darkness when Islam made its appearance, none was more ignoble and humiliated than man. Without realisation of his worth, he had no sense of human dignity. A sacred tree or animal, dedicated to some religious belief or practice, enjoyed a more coveted place than man himself. Human sacrifice on the altars of countless deities was a common spectacle. It was solely through Muhammad the Prophet, peace be upon him, that men came to appreciate the fact that human beings, the glorious creation of God, were entitled to much more loving regard, respect and honour than any other creature. The rank accorded to man was next only to God, for God had Himself heralded the purpose of man's creation in words of lasting beauty:

> He it is who created for you all that is in the earth. (al-Baqara, 2: 29)

Man was declared as the best of creations, the ruler of the

world and all that existed in it:

> Verily We have honoured the children of Adam. We carry
> them on the land and the sea, and have made provision of
> good things for them, and have preferred them above many of
> those whom We created with a marked preferment (*al-Isrā'*,
> 17: 70)

A celestial Tradition of the Prophet, peace be upon him,
alludes to the deep concern of God for the welfare of human
beings. As narrated fully in the last chapter, (p. 85) it
describes how God will question regarding the sick, the
hungry and the thirsty, as if to neglect their care was
tantamount to neglecting God himself.

Islam preaches unalloyed and absolute unity of God and
rejects every form of anthropomorphism. Even so, it can
employ this analogy to drive home the rank and dignity of
man in the eyes of God. Has any other religion or
philosophical thought accorded a nobler place to human
beings than Islam?

The Prophet of Islam, peace be upon him, stressed the
importance of right actions in attracting the blessings of God.
Most praiseworthy were kindness and consideration from one
man to another.

> The Most Compassionate (God) is kind to those who are kind
> to others. If you would show kindness to those who live on
> the earth, He who lives in the Heaven shall shower His
> blessings on you.

The condition of mankind when this powerful voice was
raised in the world was pitiable. Human life was of little
account. Rulers diced with the lives of their subjects as they
chose: a man was subject to his master's whim. For centuries
the world had been one vast battlefield where kings and
emperors fought for supremacy with the lives of their
subjects. The entire population of a conquered land could be
put to the sword at the hand of the victor.

In addition a profound sense of pessimism springing from
the worthlessness of human nature and hopelessness of
Divine succour filled the air. The ancient religions of the East
and the perverted form of Christianity in the West, both had

a share in producing a climate of despair. The philosophy of reincarnation preached by the ancient religion of India assigned no place to the will and decision of man in shaping his destiny. This present life was but a form of retribution for his actions during his previous life. The Christian doctrines of original sin and atonement had joined hands to shake man's confidence all over the world in the determination and accountability of human actions. Mankind had lost faith in the mercy of God. His eternal and immutable decrees seemed to condemn man to a predetermined destiny in which his own conduct, good or bad, was of little consequence. But Muhammad, peace be upon him, affirmed that man was born with a clean slate and perfect freedom of action. He was, declared the Prophet, the author of his actions, both good and evil. As such he was solely responsible for his deeds, and would earn reward or punishment according to his deserts. Discarding the theory of vicarious atonement, the Qur'ān established the principle, once and for all, that every man was his own redeemer.

> And that man hath only that for which he maketh effort. And that his effort will be seen. (*al-Najm,* 53: 39-40)

This was the message of salvation which gave man a new confidence as master of his own destiny. He could apply himself with renewed vigour, confidence and determination to shaping his own life and re-forming the future of humanity.

The doctrine of forgiveness of sins was one of the most bounteous gifts of Islam to mankind. The Prophet, peace be upon him, declared that sins were but temporary deviations from the right path inherent in the nature of man, and were brought about by ignorance, mistake, man's own desire and the promptings of the devil. But man's deeper desire was to regret his mistakes and seek pardon of God with a contrite heart. To be broken in spirit by a sense of guilt and to seek forgiveness of God showed the innate goodness of human nature and attracted the mercy of God. This gospel of hope and good tidings was a revolutionary message to despondent humanity condemned for ever by the guilt of original sin and past misdeeds. How profound a change it wrought on the prevailing atmosphere of gloom and depression is illustrated by the fact that the Prophet, peace be upon him, came to be known as the 'Apostle of Repentance'. Repentance, he said, did not involve faint-heartedness, nor did it arise from fear of disapprobation, but was a bold and daring step taken by the first man Adam, which showed the innate nobility of his nature. Repentance was sanctified as one of the acts of devotion due to God. So forcefully did the Prophet, peace be upon him, preach the virtue of repentance, that even those who seemed irredeemably sunk in sin turned in repentance to God and attained a sublimity of spirit that was envied by others.

Describing the clemency of God which is ever willing to forgive sinners, the Qur'ān speaks with such alluring charm that one wonders whether God loves best those who seek His forgiveness after deviating from the path of virtue. God's magnanimity to those who turn to Him for forgiveness, is endless; He is forgiving and of great mercy. In the words of the Qur'ān:

> Say: O my slaves who have been prodigal to their own hurt! Despair not of the mercy of Allah, who forgiveth all sins. Lo! He is the Forgiving, the Merciful. (*al-Zumar*, 39: 53)

Other verses in the Qur'ān exhort believers to acquire positive merit and win everlasting bliss:

> And vie one with another for forgiveness from your Lord, and for a Paradise as wide as are the heavens and the earth, prepared for those who ward off (evil).

> Those who spend (of that which Allah hath given them) in ease and in adversity, those who control their wrath and are forgiving toward mankind; Allah loveth the good.

> And those who, when they do an evil thing or wrong them-selves, remember Allah and implore forgiveness for their sins — Who forgiveth sins, save Allah only? — and will not knowingly repeat (the wrong) they did.

> The reward of such will be forgiveness from their Lord, and Gardens underneath which rivers flow, wherein they will abide for ever — a bountiful reward for workers! (*Āl 'Imrān*, 3: 133-5)

Among the characteristics of the true believer enumerated in another verse, repentance takes precedence over all others.

> (Triumphant) are those who turn repentant (to Allah) those who serve (Him), those who praise (Him), those who fast, those who bow down, those who fall prostrate (in worship), those who enjoin the right and who forbid the wrong and those who keep the limits (ordained) of Allah — and give glad tidings to believers? (*al-Tawba*, 9: 112)

The place of honour accorded to those who repent of their sins is further illustrated by those verses of the Qur'ān revealed on the occasion of the forgiveness of three Companions of the Holy Prophet, peace be upon him, who had been excluded from other followers for their failure to accompany him on the expedition to Tabūk. Before the verses alluding to the mistake of these Companions being condoned by God, the Qur'ān mentions the Prophet, peace be upon him, and the *Anṣār* and *Muhājir* Companions in order that no stigma may remain attached to them after their mistake had been pardoned. The Qur'ān in this way, teaches all believers who take the Companions of the Prophet, peace be upon him, as models of virtue, that no ignominy attaches to a man after a genuine change of heart:

> Allah hath turned in mercy to the Prophet, and to the *Muhājirīn* and the *Anṣār* who followed him in the hour of hardship.
> After the hearts of a party of them had almost swerved aside, then turned He unto them in mercy. Lo! He is Full of pity, Merciful for them.
>
> And to the three also (did He turn in mercy) who were left behind, when the earth, vast as it is, was straitened for them, and their own souls were straitened for them till they bethought them that there is no refuge from Allah save toward Him. Then turned He unto them in mercy that they (too) might turn (repentant unto Him). Lo! Allah! He is the Relenting, the Merciful! (*al-Tawba*, 9: 117-118)

Remission of sin leads us to one of the chief attributes of

101

the Divine Being — His mercy and compassion. The bounty of God's mercy is the constant theme of the Qur'ān. Says God: 'My mercy embraces all things'. (*al-A'rāf*, 7: 156), while a celestial Tradition of the Prophet tells us: 'Verily my Mercy overcomes My anger'. To despair of God's mercy was made a cardinal sin. Quoting Jacob and Ibrāhīm, two great Prophets of God, the Qur'ān announces:

> Verily none despair of the comfort of Allah except a people disbelieving. (*Yūsuf*, 12: 87)

and:

> Who despaireth of the mercy of his Lord save those who are astray? (*al-Ḥijr*, 15: 56)

According to the Jewish and Christian doctrines, the misery and suffering of humanity on earth was but a feeble image of the never ending agony which awaited them in the future world. The medieval monastic orders developed this doctrine with appalling vividness and in graphic detail. Humanity, scared by these ghastly visions and glimpses of eternal suffering, was relieved by the Prophet's, peace be upon him, emphasis on God's all-embracing mercy and the efficacy of repentance which could wipe clean the slate of even the most vicious among the castaways of society.

UNITY OF LIFE
There is yet another gift of the prophethood of Muhammad, peace be upon him, still more far-reaching, more beneficial to humanity at large. This is the concept of the unity of spirit and matter: the harmony of the sacred and the profane. He taught that the dichotomy between the two was superficial, more apparent than real. Every one of man's actions, his behaviour and morality, is guided by his motive, which, in the terminology of religion, is known as *niyyah* or intention. No religious belief is entirely divorced from the realities of human experience in its manifold practical aspects. The intention or purpose with which any act is done is the criterion of its moral worth. The Qur'ān does not recognise any division between the temporal and the spiritual since man's desire to propitiate God and follow His

commands permeates every fibre of human activity, no matter whether it is the art of government or war; availing oneself of one's earthly possessions or satisfaction of one's natural desires; earning one's living or leading a satisfactory married life. If the intention is good even the most mundane act is turned into a virtuous deed, and becomes a means of bringing man nearer to God. On the contrary, no merit whatsoever attaches to right acts — like devotion to God or fighting in His cause — if the sincere desire to attain the will and pleasure of God is absent.

The ancient world had divided life into two compartments — the religious and the secular. As a result a wedge had been driven between those who selected one or other of these modes of life. Frequently the two groups were at loggerheads with one another, for the 'world' and 'religion' were to them incompatible spheres of human life. Every man was forced to choose one or the other, since no-one could be expected to travel in two boats at the same time. The prevalent view was that the path of salvation lay not through the rough and tumble of life, but only in isolation from the social, economic and political problems of worldly pursuits. No concept of religion which barred the gates to material progress and acquisition of power, riches and fame, could be of interest to intelligent, capable and ambitious persons. Forced by this dichotomy to choose between the world and religion, large numbers of the most able people dissociated themselves from the rigours and constraints of religious and ascetic life. By withdrawing themselves from the pursuit of virtue, such men frustrated any integration of secular and religious affairs. Morality appeared to vanish from the conduct of public affairs. The State eventually revolted against the Church and made itself free from all obligations to it. This hideous schizophrenia not only divorced what was called worldly from the benefit of spiritual wisdom, but also gave birth to the faithlessness and agnosticism of modern Europe, which is now threatening, because of its political and cultural supremacy, to inundate the entire world. The present wave of gross materialism, loss of faith and moral debasement can be seen as a direct consequence of the division between spirit and matter effected by the older civilisations. It was left to the

103

Prophet, peace be upon him, to re-integrate the spiritual and temporal spheres of life: to persuade men of religion and men of the world to unite in bringing about God's kingdom on earth.

It would be difficult to conceive a more complete transformation of life than the one brought about by the fusion of the secular and the sacred. Let us leave the last word with Iqbal, one of Islam's great poets:

> On monastic order was laid the foundation of Church,
> How could mendicity contain royalty in its confines?
> The conflict was deep between hermit and king,
> One was triumphant, the other subdued.
> Politics got rid of religion,
> Helpless was the high priest.
> When the world and religion parted ways,
> Avarice was Ruler, King and Vizier.
> Dualism was the doom of mind and matter,
> Dualism made civilization blind.
> This is the miracle of the dweller of the desert,
> Whose warnings reflected the tidings glad;
> That humanity's only refuge was this —
> That the mystic Junaid unite with Ardsher the King.

PURPOSE IN LIFE

Yet another radical change brought about by the Prophet of Islam, peace be upon him, in the life of man was to make him conscious of the ultimate end of existence. Unaware of any ultimate purpose, man had for long fixed his eyes on trivial and ephemeral ends. He directed his whole intelligence and labour to the acquisition of material wealth, fame or power. The only virtue lay in the pursuit of pleasure: happiness became identified with the satisfaction of worldly desires. But Muhammad, peace be upon him, told man that the business of mankind was to exert itself in striving to attain perfect knowledge of God; to contemplate His nature and attributes; to bring his soul nearer to God through awareness of the infinite; to seek unity in the diversity of nature; to seek fulfilment in virtuous acts. He told man that these were the objectives whose achievement conferred on him a rank envied by the angels of God.

The prophethood of Muhammad, peace be upon him, made a clean sweep of the existing order of things in the world. The desire and longing of man was now centred on a new objective. Love of God took possession of his being; the pleasure of God became the everlasting thirst of the human heart; mercy and kindness to God's creatures became the prime object of his endeavours. It was only after the advent of the Prophet, peace be upon him, that the countries who submitted to Islam adopted the pursuit of spiritual values as a way of life. In Arabia and Persia, Syria and Egypt, Turkestan and Iraq, North Africa and Spain, thousands of souls undertook the search for higher and tender virtues. During this period we find innumerable men of God preaching to all mankind love of the Lord, kindness and compassion, the merits of virtuous living, the acquisition of Divine knowledge, the rejection of cruelty and indecency, and the grace of humility and modesty. They taught the lessons of human dignity and the brotherhood of man and sought to bring about the kingdom of God on earth.

Could we today look into the hearts of these supreme examples of mankind, we would witness the depth and purity of their innermost being. We would see how they were ever willing to put their own life at stake for others, made their own children and family suffer for the good of all, compelled autocrat kings and potentates to do justice to the weak and the poor, and dispensed true justice even to their enemies. Had historians and biographers not preserved a faithful record of their lives, the truth of their deeds would be beyond belief. This revolutionary change in the manners and morals of people was indeed a miracle worked by the Holy Prophet of Islam, peace be upon him; the sum of his great gifts to mankind.

PART II

MUSLIMS
The Mission and the Community

Chapter Eight

Live as Emissaries of Islam

The petition that the Prophet, peace be upon him, made to Allah on the day of Badr was indeed a pledge and a covenant he made on behalf of his Ummah for all time to come: that they will exist solely to invite mankind to worship God alone. On the basis of this pledge they were granted victory over the forces that had come to destroy them. Had Muslims not been victorious at Badr, there would have been no Muslims today.

Every Muslim, wherever he lives, shares this pledge simply by virtue of being a Muslim. So do those who live in the West, says Nadwi. Let them not be overwhelmed by the culture that surrounds them. Let them arise with courage and faith and give a call to break all false images and idols who have usurped the lordship over man. Let them be emissaries of God and His Prophet, peace be upon him, in a world which, despite its vast progress, is faced with destruction at its own hands. Let them rise above petty, selfish considerations. Only then will their stay in an un-Islamic environment be justified. [Ed.]

THE WEST TODAY

You are Muslims. I would therefore start by impressing upon you not to be overwhelmed by Western civilisation. You are the fruit of the tree of Prophethood. Live here, but keep away from slavish imitation of the West. Derive as much benefit as you can from your stay, but do not be swayed by crude and vulgar materialism. Remember the message of Islam and be on guard against the dissolution of your personality. Do not feel ashamed of your faith and culture. Do not imagine that you are the beasts and they are men. No; you are the men, only if you are truly Muslims. This land glitters with electric lights; even the night here is bright as day; but it is devoid of true effulgence, of blessedness and Divine guidance — as Iqbal wrote:

> Dark is the Frankish country with the smoke of its machines;
> This 'valley of Blessedness and Hope' is not worthy of Divine Splendour.

The Prophet Ibrāhīm (Abraham), peace be upon him, asked the idol worshippers of his time: 'What are these images unto which ye pay devotion?' *(al-Anbiyā', 21: 52)*. What irony is it that what you yourselves make one day you kneel down before it the other day? The same is happening here. Today a theory is formulated, a law discovered, a powerful machine made; and, tomorrow, the whole nation becomes subservient to them. Bondsmen of the idols and images carved by their own hands!

This country has indeed become an idol-hall, in which the *adhān* (call) of Ibrāhīm has to be given. This you alone can do. You are the real descendants of Ibrāhīm; not the Jews who have strayed far away from his path, nor the Christians who are the followers of the Christianity of Paul, not of

---

From a speech delivered at the Muslim Community Centre, Chicago on 19 June, 1977. The first part of this speech is included in Chapter 5.

Jesus. They have been divested of true Christianity — it was a colossal tragedy that bore poisonous fruit. No religious distortion has, perhaps, been so successful. It brought about a complete metamorphosis of Christianity. Now, whether Catholics or Protestants, Christians are the adherents of Paul and have given up the claim to be the successors of Ibrāhīm. You are his true successors.

Recall the words of Iqbal:

> Architect of *Ḥaram,* for rebuilding the world awake;
> Out of heavy sleep, heavy sleep, arise.
> Out of slumber deep arise.

Only the architects of *Ḥaram* can build the new world. Today, destruction prevails. In appearance it is constructive, but in truth, destructive. It was the mission of the Prophet you follow, peace be upon him, to lead mankind away from every kind of subservience towards the service of One God alone. You, therefore, are in America not merely as flesh and blood, nor simply as Indians, Pakistanis, Egyptians, Syrians —

> Break idols of colour and blood; lose yourselves in the *Millah,*
> Neither the Irani should remain, nor Turani, nor Afghani.

— but as Muslims, one Community, one brotherhood. You are Ibrahīmī and Muhammadī. Know yourselves. You have not come here to lose your identity and get fitted into this monstrous machine or to fill your bellies like animals. No. Take the message of Islam to the peoples of this land; wake them up; tell them how they have gone astray from the right way.

Strangely enough, if it ever occurs to the Western people how wrong and perverted their outlook on life is, they go to the other extreme. They turn towards Hippie-ism, Hindu asceticism and renunciation. A large bathing festival, called *Kumbh,* is held every year at Allahabad, in India. If you go to it, you will find educated Americans roaming about like lost sheep, or, rather, lunatics. This civilisation has developed indigestion. They have imbibed the wine of their culture so excessively that they have begun to vomit. They look for

111

satisfaction by descending to the level of animals, by rejecting the favours and blessings of God, by running away from the realities of life.

Would to God that our Islamic countries were capable of showing the correct path to the Americans and speaking to them in a confident, self-assured manner. But, alas, not one of them is in that position. The result is that when the Americans get disgusted with their own way of life, they go to the Himalayas and use narcotics to produce an unreal feeling of peace and serenity. We Muslims could offer guidance to them if we but possessed the confidence in our capacity.

WHY YOU ARE HERE

Brothers and sisters, you are not here merely to earn and spend. This any community can do. You are here to earn according to your need, but you must, also, know your mission and present before the Americans a new way of life. You should call the *adhān* to stir their minds and offer *Ṣalāt* that they may see and ponder over it. Lead a clean life in order that a revulsion is created in them for their own degenerate ways of living. Practise moderation so that a realisation may come to them of the foulness and folly of excessive self-indulgence. Free yourselves from the ruthless domination of the machines, live in a cool, calm and collected manner in order that they may know where peace lies. Rediscover the world that lies within you and develop the spirituality which might be felt by those who come into contact with you. I wish that devout bondsmen of the Lord, men with illumined hearts, may come to live here and teach these people who are disgusted with life that 'Verily in the remembrance of Allah do hearts find rest' (*al-Ra'd,* 13: 28).

Today, only the Muslims can give this message, but *where* are they? Has any Muslim country or community the face to tell the Americans that 'in the remembrance of Allah do hearts find rest'? They no longer believe in it themselves. How can they convey the message of Divine Unity to others who have themselves lost faith in the efficacy of *Ṣalāt,* in the truth of the *kalima,* in the ultimate power of God over all gains and losses, and in the preordination of good and evil? How can they, who revere the Americans as the great providers of the daily bread, tell them that there is no Giver of sustenance save Allah?

First, try to create faith within yourselves; observe *Ṣalāt* and spend some time every day in meditation; generate the sensitiveness that has been dried out by the smoke of the factories; refresh your souls, set right the aim of your life; read the Qur'ān daily, study the life of the Prophet, peace be upon him, and seek light from it; and, then, convey the message of Islam to the Americans.

Islam alone is the religion that does not frown upon human nature, but declares it to be essentially pure and flawless. God gave a clean slate to man, a guiltless nature, an inclination towards goodness; we have debased it. Man is, by nature, upright; left to his natural instincts, he will follow the correct path. First, realise these truths, effect them within yourselves, in your hearts as well as in your minds, and, then, put them to the Americans.

You are people of preaching and instruction; a community with a purpose, and the bearers of the Message. It does not become you to live like two-legged animals, filling your stomachs and procreating.

I have spoken to you from the heart. I have seen everything in America, but not the 'man'. It is not that I am unacquainted with America or the Americans. I have met them also in literature, on the T.V. and over the radio. They are not strangers to me.

BE EMISSARIES OF ISLAM

If I expect to find one here, it is among you. Seek to be the 'man' who is the vicegerent of God and for whom the world has been created; in him beats the heart more precious than all the world. All the treasures of the earth and the achievements of science are as nothing before an illuminated heart. Create that humanity in yourselves.

Your stay here is correct; not only justified, but an act of worship if it is a source of preaching and propagation of faith. But if not, then I have great misgivings. As I have said on various occasions, if you do not take full care to safeguard your religious life and arrange for the religious education and upbringing of your children and make sure that your future generations remain true to Islam, then your living in this country is a sin and you are in grave danger.

> Lo! As for those whom the angels take (in death) while they wrong themselves, (the angels) will ask: In what were ye engaged? They will say: We were helpless in the land. (The angels) will say: Was not Allah's earth spacious that ye could have migrated therein? (al-Nisā', 4: 97)

For us Muslims it is permitted to live only in a country where we can live with our distinctive qualities and observe our duties. If it is not possible in this environment or you feel you cannot carry out your religious obligations, it is not permissible for you to stay. It is your duty to see that you live here distinctly as Muslims. You should build your own society and ensure that your children will remain Muslims after you, as Ya'qūb (Jacob) did in regard to his children. It is set forth in the Qur'ān:

> Or were you present when death came to Ya'qūb, when he said unto his sons: What will you worship after me? They said: We shall worship thy God, the God of thy fathers, Ibrāhīm and Ismā'īl (Ishmael) . . . (al-Baqara, 2: 133).

Only then was Ya'qūb satisfied and he departed from the world with a contented heart. It is the duty of all of us to make certain that our children grow up to be Muslims; otherwise, friends, it will be necessary to have a second look at whether you continue to live in this country or not.

I highly appreciate the services of institutions and individuals (like MSA) who strive in the cause of faith, form study circles, circulate Islamic literature and organise meetings. Whether they are Arabs or non-Arabs, they are a blessed group. God will accept their services and raise them in the ranks of the fortunate. Of foremost importance, however, is the stipulation that you make your stay here as practising Muslims and not break up or lose your identity. Would you melt like wax before the heat of this civilisation? If so, better go back to your native lands, no matter that you earned only a fourth or a fiftieth part of what you do here. And if you are safe against it and there is no such danger then

114

your stay in America is blessed: a new light may come to it through you, and the path may be opened for Islam.

Chapter Nine

If Ye are True in Faith!

The most important resource that the Muslims in the West, indeed anywhere, have to enable them to bring Islam to mankind in adverse circumstances is faith and trust in Allah. Neither power nor riches can avail if faith is missing. With faith, despair and frustration cannot exist.

Nadwi draws attention to the early era of Islam to find out how true this is. The Muslims' encounter with the Quraish of Makka, the Romans and the Persians was, materially, very unequal, but they had one thing which their opponents did not have: the wealth of faith. Before that faith all the false gods of worldly wealth and power crumbled. They set out to rescue humanity from the darkness of ignorance, superstition, servility and too many gods, and did just that! The simple, illiterate bedouins were soon the leaders of the world. Can the same thing happen today? It can, asserts Nadwi, only if Muslims have faith in their mission. That mission is eminently portrayed in the words of the Prophet, peace be upon him, at the Battle of Badr when he turned to God and said: 'If these handful of men are killed today, thou shalt not be worshipped on the earth till the Day of the Last Judgement'. [Ed.]

9

You are the hunter of the Phoenix; it is only the beginning,
The world of fish and fowl has not been created in vain.

The Qur'ān says:

> So lose not heart, nor fall into despair, for ye must gain mastery if ye are true in Faith. (*Āl 'Imrān*, 3: 139)

This verse was revealed at a time when Islam was in its infancy, and the Islamic state had not been founded. The light of faith had not at that time spread beyond the Arabian peninsula. Its people generally led a life of extreme poverty. They lived for the most part on dates, camel flesh and barley-bread; they wore rough, coarse clothes and lived in mud huts or tents. Their misery and helplessness at that time has been described in these words by the Qur'ān, than which there can be no better nor more trustworthy testimony:

> And remember, when you were few and reckoned feeble in the land and were in fear lest men should extirpate you. (*al-Anfāl*, 8: 26)

Such was the condition of the Arabs. In contrast, the Romans and the Persians enjoyed world leadership. They had built up magnificent civilisations and their writ was absolute for vast numbers of people. The Eastern and Western parts of the known world were divided between these two powers. They enjoyed immense wealth and power and all the good things of life were available to them in abundance.

SOURCE OF STRENGTH
It was in these circumstances that the Qur'ān challenged

From the Friday sermon delivered on 3 June, 1977, in the assembly rooms of the United Nations where its Muslim employees meet for the Friday Prayer.

the power-drunk nations of Rome and Persia, while at the same time infusing dignity and self-confidence into the weak, helpless Arab Muslims. It declared: 'So lose not heart, nor fall into despair; for ye must gain mastery if ye are true in Faith' (*Āl 'Imrān,* 13: 139). The Qur'ān challenged the Quraish of Makka and the Romans and Persians, and then, to comfort and console the leader of the handful of Muslims, the Prophet Muhammad, peace be upon him, *Sūra Yūsuf* was revealed. The Qur'ān proclaimed:

> For those who question, for them are signs (of Allah's sovereignty) in the life story of Yūsuf (Joseph) and his brothers. (12: 7)

The *Sūra* ends with these words:

> Till, when the Messengers despaired and thought that they were denied, then came unto them Our help, and whom We would was saved. And Our wrath cannot be warded from the guilty.

> In their history, verily, there is a lesson for men of understanding. It is no invented story but (the Qur'ān is) a confirmation of the existing (Scripture) and a detailed explanation of everything and a guidance and a mercy for those who believe. (12: 110-111)

Similarly, the promise of *Sūra al-Qaṣaṣ,* revealed against a background of oppression and fear, was to thunder in the world:

> Tā. Sīn. Mīm. These are revelations of the Scripture that maketh plain. We narrate unto thee (somewhat) of the story of Moses and Pharaoh with truth, for folk who believe.

> Lo! Pharaoh exalted himself in the earth and made its people castes. A tribe among them he oppressed, killing their sons and sparing their women. Lo! he was of those who work corruption.

> And We deemed to show favour unto those who were oppressed in the earth and to make them examples and to make them the inheritors. And to establish them in the earth, and to show Pharaoh and Hāmān and their hosts that which they feared from them. (28: 1-6)

119

Who could have dreamt of anything good in the dreadful conditions prevailing among the Arab Muslims? Who could prophesy that those destitute, empty-handed, oppressed and down-trodden Muslims would shine on the firmament of history? No wise or sensible person, however gifted with foresight, could have said to that handful of men: *So lose not heart, nor fall into despair; for ye must gain mastery if ye are true in Faith.*

But this exhortation filled the Muslims' hearts with such courage and enthusiasm that the mighty Romans and Persians appeared to them to be no more than pygmies. To quote the Qur'ān once again:

> And when thou seest them their figures please thee; and if they speak thou givest ear unto their speech. (But, in fact, they are) as though they were propped up blocks of wood. (*al-Munā-fiqūn,* 63: 4)

When the Arabs came out of their desert land, with the wealth of spirit of their faith, they cared nothing for the strength and vastness of the Roman and Persian Empires and swept over them like an irresistible tidal wave. In the words of Iqbal:

> Desert and oceans fold up at their kick,
> And mountains shrink into mustard-seeds.
> Indifferent to the riches of the world it makes,
> What a curious thing is the joy of love?

THE EARLY ARAB MUSLIMS

When the Arabs ventured forth, they were a new power, a more than natural power. They were now a unique people filled with a singular passion. They were, of course, weak and poor — no part of the earth was under their rule. But when they stepped out of Arabia, fired with the spirit of monotheism, they had begun to understand the difference between man and man, faith and unfaith, between form and reality; the contrast between the real fountain of immortality and the ideal in life which appears like a mirage of the desert became clear to them. God had endowed them with the light of faith, and therewith a firm grasp of the nature and significance of man's destiny: to eat, drink and be merry was not the high aim and purpose of his creation; his destiny lay in the Divine assurance. 'Surely We created man of the best stature'.

When the Muslims had comprehended this fundamental truth, and the reality of the world and what lay beyond it had become clear to them, false manifestations of worldly power and glory failed to impress them and the ass dressed in the tiger's skin began to look to them the ass that it was. Caesar and Chosroes were, now, no more to them than birds chattering in a cage: the cage bars were made of gold, but a cage, after all, was a cage, even if studded with diamonds, very extensive, and with ponds and orchards and stately buildings in it. The Arabs were no more impressed by those who wore crowns on their heads or were known by the dignified titles of ministers, army generals, princes and philosophers, than by actors in a play acting their high-sounding parts: for the hearts of these dignitaries were frozen, their souls dead, their minds sterile — they strove to hide their inner insolvency in vulgar ostentation and in the sycophancy of servile flatterers. The Arabs realised that these were only the figures of human beings, hollow within, lacking in conviction and strong purpose, their thoughts and activities directed towards the pleasure of the senses alone. They had no higher aim or ideal in life. There was no place for human sympathy in their calculations; human beings were only tools for the realisation of their desires and ambitions. There were crowns on their heads, but the heads were empty; and costly dresses on their bodies, but the bodies were strengthless.

When the Arabs set out with the object of rescuing humanity from the savagery and barbarism that had been going on for centuries, truth had already dawned upon them. When they set out to deliver men from bondage to their fellow men to the bondage to One God, from the narrow confines of this world to the infinite extensiveness of the Hereafter, and from the oppressiveness of their faith and creeds to the justice of Islam, the soulless pomp and splendour seemed worthless to them and the powerful empires no more than a toy house. To lower the flags of the

Romans and Persians was child's play to them. The Qur'ān had filled these illiterate, backward Arabs with ardour and strength, raised their hearts with pride, self-confidence and magnanimity. It had taught them the real worth of things, their true qualities and effects. The Arabs set out with these truths and dominated the world, but not to rule over it as other races had done. They set out to make mankind that had gone astray bow its head before One God and to bring it into the shade of Islamic justice and equity.

And we, friends, here we are, so many centuries later, at the headquarters of the United Nations. Now that we represent numerous states and governments, we are more worthy of the dignity and self-reliance that was enjoyed by the early Arab Muslims. We better deserve to be addressed by the heavenly voice which addressed them. *So lose not heart, nor fall into despair; for ye must gain mastery if ye are true in Faith.*

When this verse was revealed, there was no government of the Arabs in any part of the world — not even in the Peninsula of Arabia — Islam had made its advent barely ten years ago and it was toddling like a child. But if God found them worthy of being addressed with those soul-stirring words, do we not deserve to be recipients of that Divine exhortation today, when we represent some forty states and a large number of our flags are flying on the building of the United Nations? Though we do not possess nuclear arsenals, lag behind in scientific knowledge and modern education, though we do not come up to the level of the Western nations in many respects (because of our apathy and internal discord and failure to appreciate the true worth of the Islamic teachings), we are nevertheless in much better shape than the Arabs of the earliest decades of Islam who did not have even a state or government of their own. Don't we, then, also deserve to be told: *So lose not heart, nor fall into despair; for ye must gain mastery if ye are true in Faith.*

Conviction in this Divine promise is the real prize of a truthful believer. It is the energy cell without which a torch is worthless, the make-weight that tips the balance of the scale. It is the same make-weight that was added to the balance by the Holy Prophet, peace be upon him, when, in the thick of the Battle of Badr, he spoke these memorable words:

> O Lord! If these handful of men are killed today, Thou shalt not be worshipped on the earth till the end of time.

The Prophet, peace be upon him, realised that it was the moment for repentance and supplication. There was no future for Islam nor for the Muslims if the outcome of the Battle of Badr was going to be determined by numbers and plain strength. They would have been wiped from the face of the earth for they were only three hundred while against them was a fully equipped army one thousand strong. How could the Muslims prevail over the mighty pagans? At that critical moment, the Prophet, peace be upon him, turned to God with earnest repentance and Prayer and entreated Him: If these handful of men are killed today, Thou shalt not be worshipped on the earth till the Day of the Last Judgement.

THE ROLE OF MUSLIMS
This defines our value and role. The Islamic countries carry certain weight in the world and even in the United Nations. Were the people whom we have the honour to represent possessed of a living faith, permeating every nerve and fibre of their being the Muslims would even now be honourable in the world and command a position of strength and importance.

Brothers, do not look to anyone for aid or support. Avoid being hangers-on of others. Borrowed strength is ephemeral; it does not endure. Also let it not be that, while your name shines in the commity of nations, and, numerically, you are strong in the population count of the world, you have no weight in the scales of God. We can be weighty in the scales of God only when we are believers with the spark of true faith in our hearts; when we are the bearers, indeed proud bearers, of the message of Islam — even here, in the United States, the citadel of Western power; when we can say to the trumpet's sound that we are Muslims, an imperishable people and the custodians of the Divine message. We are not parasites or spongers. No, indeed, we possess our own culture and civilisation and we are not going to accept any grafting upon it. The Lord has bestowed upon us the greatest favour and blessing, that is Islam.

God will be our Helper and Protector when we are proud of Islam, and Islam is ours and we are of and for Islam. It is the promise of the Almighty, and Allah never breaks His promise. Says the Qur'ān:

> If ye help (in the cause of) Allah, He will help you and plant your feet firmly. (Muḥammad, 47: 7)

But if we remain Muslims only in name and the reality of Islam is not present in us, we cannot hope for any help from the Lord since it is faith alone that counts with Him and carries weight.

May Allah grant us the good fortune to revive the Islamic values in our midst and to cherish them again: to bend only before Him, and fear no one besides Him, and be loyal to His faith, and proud of His message! We beseech Him from the depths of our hearts to confer this wealth upon us. He, indeed, is Able to do all things.

Chapter Ten

Main Duty of Muslim Immigrants

Most of the Muslim immigrants living in the West today have come for economic ends. Yet, for the Muslim, there can be only one end in life: to worship One God. Whether one lives in his native land is not important, though Nadwi suggests that the consequences of such a large number of talented Muslims living outside their own countries must be seriously considered. What is really important is that the purpose of life must be fulfilled. Only staying in that land shall be blessed where that purpose is being fulfilled. Indeed, under certain circumstances, it becomes obligatory for one to leave his native land.

Muslims in the West should therefore consider it their main duty to ensure that they live as Muslims and their children are raised as Muslims. Having migrated to earn money is no sin, it can even be beneficial. Muslim traders succeeded in bringing the message of Islam to vast numbers of people on the coasts of Africa, India and in the Far East.

Indeed Muslims can make their stay in the West a Jihād, *if they ceaselessly pursue the objective of safeguarding their Islamic identity and values, of raising their children as Muslims, of communicating the message of Islam to their neighbours. Children deserve special attention; a few hours every day must be set aside for them.* [Ed.]

10

AIM OF LIFE

> O My bondsmen who believe! spacious is My earth, therefore serve ye Me (and Me alone). (al-'Ankabūt, 29: 56)

The aim of man's existence, in the sight of God, is submission, that is, to attain a true awareness of God, to conduct his life in conformity with God's commands, to seek God by following the path laid down by the Blessed Prophet, peace be upon him, and to make provision for the Hereafter. This is the real aim; all other things are the means to it. You, of course, know the significance of ends and means. The seeking out of ways of gaining nearness to God, the creation of a suitable climate for this and the development of a critical sense that makes it easy rather than difficult to observe the God-given laws. Finally, there should be no question of compulsion nor of any other power to obtrude or give a parallel call — the Qur'ān alludes to this in the words:

> . . . Until there is no more tumult or oppression, and there prevail justice and faith in Allah. (al-Baqara, 2: 193)

This refers to a state where Truth is triumphant and no battles are waged for the souls of men and they do not have to undergo the ordeal of deciding which way to turn; where only God is obeyed and Divine honours are paid to Him alone; where justice and faith in Allah prevail. For that state, there is preaching, the sanctioning of what is right and forbidding of what is wrong, and, if need be, even Jihād. For that state, Islam is to be made stronger and brought into power and authority so that even for the faint-hearted people it might not be so hard to follow the way indicated by Allah, people otherwise despairing because the way was beyond their endurance.

From a speech delivered at Toronto on 10 June, 1977.

So, the ultimate end is worship of Allah. 'I created the jinn and humankind only that they might worship Me' (*al-Dhāriyāt,* 51: 56).

Let us be clear about this, for I have noticed a good deal of confusion on this point in Europe and America, where there is a failure to distinguish between ends and means. The aim, simply, is to earn the good pleasures of the Lord. Our intention ought to be to spend in His way the life and capabilities He has granted us so that the object of life is fulfilled — God is pleased with us on the Day of Resurrection and favours us with nearness to Him and we attain the highest place in Paradise. This is the real aim. If it is being realised anywhere then blessed is the place, and if it is not being realised even in one's native land, it should be left for good. Home, parents, wives, children, kinsmen, property, trade — everything must fade into significance before duty to God. No worldly attachments should be allowed to stand in its way.

> Say: If your fathers, and your sons, and your brethren and your wives, and your tribe, and the wealth ye have acquired, and merchandise for which ye fear that there will be no sale, and dwellings ye desire are dearer to you than Allah, and His Messenger and striving in His way: then wait till Allah bringeth His command to pass. Allah guideth not wrong-doing folk. (*al-Tawba,* 9: 24)

The charm and attractiveness of Makka is proverbial. We learn from the Qur'ān that when the Prophet Ibrāhīm (Abraham), peace be upon him, had settled his helpless wife and infant child in that uncultivable valley, he made the Prayer: 'So incline some hearts of men that they may yearn towards them' (*Ibrāhīm,* 14: 37). The Prayer was granted in all respects. Overpowering, really, is the beauty and loveliness of the city of Makka where there is the Ka'ba, the well of Zam Zam, the hills of Safā and Marwa, and, close to it, Minā and 'Arafāt.

But when the Holy Prophet, peace be upon him, felt that it was becoming extremely difficult for the Muslims to worship God in that wonderful place, he told them to migrate to

Abyssinia. He did so in order that they could and should lead their lives in conformity with the faith. The Prophet, peace be upon him, observed: 'You cannot worship God here; you cannot offer Prayer: you are forced to bow your heads before the idols; God is treated with insolence in your presence: so, migrate to Abyssinia'. Twice the Muslims moved out to Abyssinia. Finally, the Prophet himself, peace be upon him, was commanded to leave Makka and go to Madina.

If a city like Makka could be abandoned so that God could be worshipped in freedom, what remains to be said of other towns, be it New York, London, Toronto, Chicago, Delhi, Lucknow, Kufa, Basra, Cordova, Granada, Cairo or Damascus. Only that place is beautiful and worth living in where the commands of the Lord can be observed, and where it is not possible, even if that is one's native land, it should be left for good.

LIVE AS MUSLIMS

Brothers! I have travelled through the United States, seeing a number of its cities. Now I am here in Canada. Of course, it has pleased me to see Muslims from different countries living in North America, and yet I wonder if you can lead a fully Islamic life here. Will it be possible for your descendants to remain true to Islam? Will the Islamic spirit abide in you undiminished? It is a serious matter. Do not take offence.

Many of you have come here for financial reasons. A brother told me plainly, 'We have come here to earn our livelihood'. It is not sinful. There is no harm in going to a place where a purely materialistic way of life prevails and utter indifference as to the Hereafter, but the decision to settle down there permanently requires careful consideration.

If you are confident that you can live here in conformity with the will of God, and you are being useful to Islam, and are safeguarding your own faith as well as caring for the faith of others, and are, also, engaged in economic activities according to your needs, then it is all right, and I will even say that your stay is propitious. God may take from you the task of spreading the guidance in this land and, one day, it might adopt Islam. It is not inconceivable. When the Muslim traders arrived in the Far East, whole countries were

128

converted to Islam and the Muslims are in a majority in Malaysia and Indonesia and in so many islands of the Indian Ocean even today. If you care to enquire, you will discover that Islam spread mainly through the efforts of the Arab traders or the Sufi-saints. In my own subcontinent, vast areas like Sind, Kashmir and Bangladesh are indebted to the Sufi saints for their conversion to Islam.

Your stay here is not only justified, but also a *Jihād* if you have made sure of the preservation of Islam for yourselves and your future generations, and are carrying out the duty of the preaching and propagation of faith and presenting an image of the Islamic way of life which is attractive to others. But in case it is otherwise and your aim is simply to make money, then it falls much short of the Islamic ideal. It is not worthy of a Muslim to undertake such a long voyage only for financial gain.

The Lord is the Giver of sustenance, and His giving is not bound by geographical limits. I am speaking to you in a practical vein. All this is related wholly to action and practice. You can hear the intellectual subtleties at some other time and from some other student of theology. I am only speaking to you in a straightforward way in the light of what I have seen here.

HOW STAYING IN THE WEST CAN BE JUSTIFIED

I declare unequivocally that if your life and your stay here are beneficial to Islam your migration is not only justifiable but also an act of worship. But if your faith and the religious life of your children are not assured, I shudder at it. I shudder at the thought in what state death might come, and then, should we tell God that we came here only to earn our livelihood? Such a motive is not in the Islamic character; it does not befit a Muslim. If you have taken due care that your faith remains unblemished, and you are associated with some religious endeavour, and have built up an Islamic environment or founded a circle in which religious activities are promoted and the Lord is remembered and attention is paid to the life of the Hereafter, and you have, also, arranged for the religious instruction of your children, then you have my sincere good wishes.

129

This last thing is very important, for when, on the Day of Judgement, the children will be asked in what miserable state they have come that they know neither the name of God nor of His Prophet, they will reply: 'Our Lord: we obeyed our chiefs and our great ones, and they misled us as to the (right) path' (al-Aḥzāb, 33: 67).

The Qur'ān says:

> O ye who believe; Ward off from yourselves and your families a Fire whereof the fuel is men and stones. (al-Taḥrīm, 66: 6)

Your children will, of course, be going to school, but do set aside for them a couple of hours in which they can receive religious instruction and learn about God and His Messenger, without which no one can be a Muslim, and let it be impressed upon them that it is sinful to die in another way than Islam: 'Die not save as men who have surrendered (unto Him)' (al-Baqara, 2: 132).

Forgive my plain speaking, but these are some practical things you must give heed to after taking up residence in this country. If you devote a little of your time to the religious education of your children and to the creation of an Islamic atmosphere, then live and prosper here by all means. Maybe, God has sent you to this land for a noble purpose.

Otherwise, I doubt even this much, even this much is uncertain, that a Muslim who dies here will be buried according to the Islamic rites. A relation of mine called Mudassir, who is settled in Boston, related to me how he was asked to take part in the last rites for a Hājī who had died. On reaching there, he found that the Hājī's body, dressed in a Western suit, complete with neck-tie and wearing a gold ring, had been placed in a wooden chest, and Christian men and women were coming in, kissing the body and placing wreaths on the coffin. May God bless Mudassir with a long life — education in the Arabic madrasas, after all, bears fruit — he took the Hājī's son aside and told him that he was leaving. 'Why?' asked the Hājī's son. Upon this he said, 'Will you do what I tell or not?' The Hājī's son replied, 'I requested your presence and will act on your advice'. 'Then', said Mudassir, 'first of all, take off the suit and tell these people to go away from here, I will bathe the dead body and cover it with a shroud as prescribed by the *Sharī'ah.* And, also, remove the ring'. 'Do not remove the ring', exclaimed the Hājī's son, otherwise my mother will die of shock'. 'I shall take off the ring', replied Mudassir, 'if you fear that your mother will die of heart failure, don't tell her now'. After much persuasion, the Hājī's son agreed and the ring was removed.

A young man educated in our *madrasas,* in our schools, happened to be by, otherwise God alone knows how many Muslims are buried here in that way.

Another similar incident that has come to my knowledge concerns an Egyptian scholar who was also the author of a book on Islam in English. He had an American wife. When he died, he was buried in a Christian cemetery as the Muslim graveyard was some distance away.

Events such as these are so horrifying that if a Muslim saw them even in a dream, he would scream out, 'Oh God! Have mercy on me'. Shame upon us that they become common and we remain unmoved.

So, brothers, have a care for yourselves and for your children, and see to it that they remain Muslims. Otherwise your immigration makes no sense to me. You are in danger and so is your country. Had the brain drain not continued unchecked and the young men, who are coming here to settle down from India and Pakistan, stayed back, they would have been a source of strength to their communities, to their parents. The number of Arabs in America is increasing day by day. They might have proved a great asset to their native lands if they had decided not to migrate. Coming here merely for larger salaries and better living conditions is beyond my comprehension. It is a question to which serious thought must be given.

Chapter Eleven

Create a Universal Islamic Society

Islam has a distinctive character of its own. This character comprehends every aspect of life — words and deeds and attitudes.

Islam also has a very sensitive temperament. It cannot assimilate ideas and institutions which are alien to it. Obviously the dangers for those who live in an un-Islamic environment, like those living in Europe and America, are serious. They are constantly in danger of being lost in the sea of an alien culture. Their Islamic identity is always susceptible to changes.

To preserve the distinctive character and temperament of Islam requires great effort. It is essential to remain on guard against the dangers of developing regional versions of Islamic culture.

This struggle requires an Islamic environment, a network of personal relationships, a conscious effort to adopt an Islamic mode of living. [Ed.]

11

Brother Muslims and friends, it is my good fortune to meet you in this great Islamic Centre. This is my first visit to North America. Before this I used to read and hear about this land and the progress Islam was making in it. I had, also, some knowledge of the religious inclination and solicitude of the Muslims who had taken up residence here. But I did not imagine that I would be meeting so many of my religious brethren in this far-off country or witnessing such a keen interest and enthusiasm for Islam.

On coming here I realised that Islam was trying to obtain a foothold in the United States which enjoys the position of leadership in the contemporary world owing, largely, to its phenomenal advances in the fields of science and industry. By the grace of God, Islam has made its debut in this part of the world and is making steady headway, and, God willing, the day is not far off when an Islamic society will be established here.

DISTINCTIVE CHARACTER OF ISLAM

It is, of course, a good augury for Islam and a matter of joy for the Muslims, but I have also some misgivings by reason of what little knowledge I possess of history. The establishment of an Islamic society so far away from the centres of Islamic faith and civilisation is open to grave risks and can lead to catastrophic consequences. Dr. Sulaiman Duniya, from whose writings I too have profited, has very aptly remarked that Islam is not exclusive to any country. I wholly agree that Islam is not a territorial faith, yet it also

---

From a speech delivered at the Islamic Centre of New Jersey on 4 June, 1977. Introducing the speaker, the Egyptian scholar, Dr. Sulaiman Duniya eulogised the services of Indian Muslims to the Arabic language and Islamic sciences and said that non-Arab Muslims had taken an equal if not greater part with the Arabs in the propagation and preservation of Islam, claiming that it transcended geographical and political boundaries.

needs a distinctive environment, a congenial climate, and a predisposition that may transcend personal, cultural and intellectual standards. It requires an Islamic homeland for it is neither a mystical doctrine nor a philosophy nor a collection of soulless beliefs and rituals, but a real, living and all-embracing faith.

Islam is comprehensive of idea and action, morality and monetary exchange, of emotion and intellect. In the same way, it is also a special inclination of human nature and a peculiar state of mind. It embraces all the manifold aspects of human personality — spiritual and material, moral and physical, emotional and intellectual, and personal and social. Whoever embraces Islam with an open heart and believing it to be the chosen faith of the Lord and the last of the Divine messages will get cast into a new mould — the mould of *islam*. He will be born anew, because Islam is a complete and eternal plan of life which comprehends all the aspects of change and revolution, and perfection and beauty. Islam is not a wooden dogma or a traditional religion, but a faith that permeates the inmost recesses of the heart and soul.

If the true image of Islam is kept in mind, evidently it is not something that can be communicated simply through the written or spoken word; it also requires a particular way of thinking, and a distinctive state of feeling. Hence, it passes judgement about the goodness and badness, desirability and undesirability of things it is related to as the Prophet, peace be upon him, is reported to have liked or disliked many things. He, for example, liked to begin every good act with the right hand, so much so that he started combing his hair from the right side or when he put on shoes, began with the right foot. Similarly, there were many things that gave him pleasure or made him annoyed and uncomfortable. Islam, in fact, is a prophetic way of life that has come down from the heavens and the Divine messengers have been its bearers and custodians, and they have left it behind as their legacy.

This is why God has described Islam as *ṣibghatullāh* (colour of Allah). Were it only a body of doctrines or a code of conduct it would not have been called *ṣibgha,* which denotes its distinct and pervasive nature. This distinguishing feature is evident when Islam draws a clear line of demarcation between one man and another, between one life, character and temperament and another life, character and temperament, and brings out clearly the difference between life-standards and values. The criterion of Islam is quite different from the criterion of non-Islam or infidelity. Hence, you will find warnings in the compilations of the Traditions and *Sunna* of the Prophet against the Age of Ignorance and its practices. For instance, sometimes, it is said about a thing that it is a practice of the Age of Ignorance (*Jāhiliyya*), and sometimes that it is very much like the bigotry and arrogance of those days.

Why does the Qur'ān call upon the Muslim women, when the Age of Ignorance had ended long ago: 'Bedizen not yourselves with the Bedizenment of the Time of Ignorance' (*al-Aḥzāb,* 33: 33)? Because ignorance was a definite way of life and had its own values and standards for judging the goodness and badness, lawfulness and unlawfulness of things, and it was a way of life which the Lord viewed with disfavour. It is mentioned in the Traditions that 'God looked at the earth and was displeased with the Arabs who dwelt on it except for a few People of the Scripture'. He disliked ignorance and therefore declared it to be undesirable for His servants.

Allah also said, 'When the unbelievers got up in their hearts heat and cant: the heat and cant of Ignorance' (*al-Fatḥ,* 48: 26). Again that is why whenever the Prophet, peace be upon him, noticed a trait of ignorance in a Muslim, he took exception to it, saying: 'You are still under the influence of Ignorance'. For instance, when he saw an illustrious Companion like Abu Dharr Ghifārī ill-treating his slave and beating him, the Prophet, peace be upon him, observed: 'The inclination towards Ignorance has not yet gone out of you'. The worthy Companion, on his part, was so deeply affected by the rebuke that he at once started treating his slave like an equal and gave him to eat and wear what he ate and wore himself.

Had Islam not possessed a distinctive character and temperament, the Lord would not have used the idea *ṣibgha,* colour, in respect of it.

The colour of Allah: and who is better than Allah at colouring. (*al-Baqara,* 2: 138)

Exhorting further His servants, the Muslims, to follow the Prophets, the Lord proclaimed, giving out a long and lustrous list of Divine Messengers:

> And We bestowed upon him Isaac and Jacob; each of them We guided; and Noah did We guide aforetime; and of his seed (We guided) David and Solomon and Job and Joseph and Moses and Aaron. Thus do We reward the Good.

> And Zachariah and John and Jesus and Elias. Each one (of them) was of the righteous.

> And Ishmael and Elisha and Jonah and Lot. Each one of them did We prefer above (Our) creatures, with some of their forefathers and their offspring and their brethren; and We chose them and guided them unto a Straight Path. Such is the guidance of Allah wherewith He guideth whom He will of His bondsmen. But if they set up (for worship) aught beside Him, all that they did would have been in vain . . . Those are they whom Allah guideth, so follow their guidance. (*al-An'ām,* 6: 85-91)

Afterwards, the Lord declared that the directive to follow was to be exclusively with regard to the Prophet Muhammad, peace be upon him, whose life was a perfect model for mankind and an ideal example. The following words were, thus, addressed to the Believers through the Holy Prophet, peace be upon him:

> Say, (O Muhammad, to mankind): If you love Allah, follow me; Allah will love you and forgive you your sins. (*Āl 'Imrān,* 3: 31)

Islam is more sensitive than any other faith. It may be enough for one to call oneself a Christian or Hindu and thereafter adopt whatever social, cultural or intellectual standards one likes. A friend of mine once said to an educated Hindu gentleman, 'My brother, if a Muslim is asked who is a Muslim, he unhesitatingly replies that whoever recites and believes in the holy *kalima* — *Lā ilāha illallāh, Muhammadur rasūlullāh,* is a Muslim. This affirmation sums

137

up the whole of Islam. Now, what would your answer be if the same question was put to you concerning a Hindu? I do not want a long and exhaustive reply because there are enough books in my library by the help of which one can understand the Brahmin or Vedantic philosophy. I have only a few minutes to spare and I want you to explain Hinduism quickly'. My friend related that the Hindu gentleman paused for a while and then said: 'A Hindu can believe or refuse to believe in anything. If a person calls himself a Hindu, he is a Hindu, and after that, it does not matter what he believes in or rejects. He remains a Hindu'.

But it is not the same with Islam. As I have said, it is a highly sensitive faith and is more quickly corrupted by things inimical to it than any other religion. Its limits are marked out very clearly. It leaves no one in doubt about itself. In concrete, well-defined and clear-cut terms, it makes it known that this is Islam and this is infidelity; this is Islam and this is ignorance; this is lawful and this is forbidden; and this is where Islam ends and infidelity and apostasy begins. Such an explicit concept of apostasy, perhaps, does not exist in any other faith. In Islam, to be an apostate is a mortal sin, the very thought of which makes one shudder. It is stated in a Tradition that 'the sign of perfection in faith is that the idea of going back to apostasy, after a man has embraced Islam, is as repugnant to him as being thrown into the fire'.

NEED OF AN ISLAMIC ENVIRONMENT

Given that the disposition of Islam is so and not otherwise, the responsibility of the Muslims who are settled in Europe or America becomes much greater. Had Islam, like the other faiths, been only a body of rites and rituals, it would have been different, but as Islam is a 'colour' and a programme of life, as it stands so insistently for a condition of feeling and awareness and requires a fundamental change in life-values and ideals — as Islam is thus and not otherwise — the responsibility of Muslims settled in Europe and America is a complex and serious matter.

We cannot, therefore, rest content with reading books and treatises, however weighty they may be. Books, of course, are necessary but we cannot cultivate the Islamic spirit wholly through them, nor develop sufficiently the Islamic mood and temperament. Our real need is an Islamic region, an Islamic 'colouring' and an Islamic environment in which we can see, hear and feel Islam directly. Personal contacts, social intercourse and the adoption of the Islamic mode of living — these are its essential conditions. We should go where the Islamic way of life and Islamic society are present in some distinct measure, where we can experience Islam as a living force.

The company of Muslims and truthful believers is so necessary that the Qur'ān advises even the Prophet, peace be upon him, whose life was a model of perfection, to seek the company of servants, pious and devoted:

> Restrain thyself along with those who cry unto their Lord at morn and evening seeking His countenance; and let not thine eyes overlook them, desiring the pomp of the life of the world; and obey not that man whose heart We have made heedless of Our remembrance, who follows his own lust and whose case has been abandoned. (al-Kahf, 18: 28)

When such was the advice to the Blessed Prophet, we can imagine how important it must be for ordinary Muslims like us to spend our time with the truthful and the pure in heart. and the pure in heart.

> O ye who believe! Be careful of your duty to Allah, and be with the truthful. (Al-Tawba, 9: 119)

The Islamic society here is in the initial stages of development and we must not neglect our duty towards it. I am confident that by the grace of God, this infant society will not only survive but flourish and mature; and that the means and opportunities of training and discipline — which are nothing but faith, study and investigation, learning and culture, and good company and shared exertion — will be available to it. Those who make sincere efforts for the glory of the Divine faith, for them the Lord opens the doors of wisdom, faith and discernment that are beyond human imagination.

> And for those who strive in Us, We surely guide them to Our paths, and lo, Allah is with the good. (al-'Ankabūt, 29: 69)

CREATE A TRULY ISLAMIC SOCIETY

Such, in brief, are the responsibilities you owe to the society you have founded in this country. It would never have come into existence had you not migrated to America and taken up residence here. You should now also take care to ensure that it develops into a truly Islamic society and does not remain confined to the ideological sphere alone because, as we know, Islam is not merely a social, political or economic concept, but, before all else, an indivisible and indissoluble creed that permeates the whole of life. It is a state of mind and a design of life. The Islam of the holy Companions possessed all these attributes. Hence, it was said by 'Abdullāh ibn Mas'ūd that 'what the Muslims consider good is good also in the judgement of God'. According to the authorities, the word 'Muslims' here denotes the Companions. It will, thus, mean that what the Companions hold to be good is good also in the sight of the Lord and what they, collectively, regard as bad is bad.

Islam and the Qur'ān demand of Muslims that they be the standard-bearers of truth and virtue. They should possess a genuine Islamic disposition so that the Americans, here, can distinguish clearly between their own society, which is being driven mercilessly by materialism, and an Islamic society which is pure, healthy and dignified — a society which spends its nights in prayer and repentance and days in seeking honest sustenance and rendering selfless service to mankind.

The creation of such a society will lead constructively to the victory of Islam. Observing it the Americans will remark that the real joy of living is in the Islamic society and not their own, they will be drawn instinctively towards it and away from the environment, literally a stinking environment, in which they were brought up.

BEWARE OF LOCAL 'ISLAMS'

I also fear the day, in America as elsewhere, if we should withdraw into ourselves and get bound up in the labyrinth of study and research; the links will be broken which connect us to the real fountainhead of Islam and to the Islamic centres where, in spite of all drawbacks, Islam is still alive, and the vital springs of eagerness for faith will dry up within us. It will then be that the American Islam, the European Islam, and the Japanese, Iranian, Indian and Pakistani Islam will emerge, as different from each other as an American is from an Asian, or a Japanese from an Afghan, and Islamic societies will appear whose mental attitudes and natural inclinations and values are widely apart.

We should take up the challenge and get ready to meet the threat now when things have not gone too far and the Islamic leaders are, to some extent, active and effective. The wisdom behind the obligatoriness of the *Hajj* (Pilgrimage), the congregation of Muslims, with all their different social, cultural and linguistic characteristics, at one particular place and one particular time, is that nothing about faith should remain vague or unclear, that stock should be taken, at one time, of all the Muslims of the world and of any local innovations and un-Islamic influences they might have accepted owing to the negligence and apathy of the *'ulamā'* or as a result of living for a considerable length of time together with other peoples and communities, and so that measures might be worked out for the eradication of un-Islamic practices. As Shāh Walīullāh so admirably put it, 'Had the *Hajj* not been there, the Islamic faith and the Muslims of the East and the West would have been the victims of change and alteration, like the other religions, and it would not have been discovered for ages'.

So, fellow Muslims, beware of the emergence of a local or territorial Islam and the establishment of Islamic societies that are devoid of the spirit of Islam and built upon foundations that are not genuinely Islamic. Believe me, this problem is not a figment of my imagination. I attach the highest importance to it, and, I am sure, when you go home and think it over you will appreciate the gravity and magnitude of the danger I have indicated.

Chapter Twelve

Faith, the Basis of Love

An enduring and strong brotherhood, based on love and trust, can exist on the basis of a strong faith in Allah. The only cementing force that can bind them in such strong, warm and cohesive relationships is loving for the sake of Allah. Love creates qualities like kindness, compassion, forgiveness, sacrifice, help and aid in need, and also checks actions which rot and corrode interpersonal relations.

The springs of love well up in hearts; no external means can penetrate those hearts. The only force that can permeate deeply into hearts is faith in Allah. To create faith and love in Allah one must make a profound study of the life of the Prophet, peace be upon him. [Ed.]

12

Today's subject is 'Mutual relations among those who work for the propagation and preservation of Islam'. I will try to shed some light on this, but my main purpose is to show what the real origin of these bonds and sentiments is.

I believe that love and fellowship cannot be generated among workers engaged in *da'wah* through external means. No substance has yet been discovered that can join human hearts — the springhead of love is found within the heart itself. Nothing in the world can unite the hearts which do not feel drawn towards each other or are not governed by a shared feeling. It is not like joining stones in a building or sticking pieces of paper together. Says the Qur'ān:

> If thou hadst spent all that is in the earth thou couldst not have attuned their hearts (i.e. the hearts of the Believers). (*al-Anfāl*, 8: 63)

Unity among the Believers could not have been produced by any means whatsoever, no matter how costly, had not God joined their hearts.

As you are aware, when the Muslims migrated from Makka to Madina there was nothing in common between the *Muhājirs*[1] and the *Anṣār*[2] except the Arabic language. Even racially they were different from one another. The *Muhājirs* belonged to the Arabian tribes of Banī 'Adnān and the *Anṣār* to the Yeminite tribes of Banī Qaḥṭān. Yet a great accord and feeling of oneness was created between them.

---

1 Literally, the 'emigrants'. Here it denotes the Muslims of Makka who had migrated to Madina and taken up residence there.

2 Literally, the 'helpers'. In Islamic terminology it applies to the inhabitants of Madina who first embraced the Islamic faith and extended warm support and hospitality to the emigrants from Makka.

From a speech delivered at the 15th Convention of the Muslim Students' Association of the United States and Canada. The audience included educationalists, writers, historians and economists.

Concerning this, the Qur'ān says:

> And remember Allah's favour unto you: how ye were enemies and He made friendship between your hearts so that ye became as brothers by His grace. (*Āl 'Imrān,* 3: 103)

It was the miracle of this brotherly feeling that when the *Muhājirs* reached Madina, the *Ansar* settled them not only in their homes, but also in their hearts. The *Ansār* said to the *Muhājirs:* 'This is my house: half of it is mine and half of it is yours. Take whichever part you like'. In the same way, the *Ansār* willingly agreed to give half of their agricultural lands and other property to the *Muhājirs,* so much so that some among them who had two wives were ready to divorce one so that their *Muhājir* brothers might marry them. And the *Muhājirs* responded with restraint and dignity. Instead of seizing greedily what was offered, they said to the *Ansār:* 'Brothers, may God grant you an increase in your riches. Show us the way to the market and we will try our luck there'.

Such warmth and earnestness, obviously, cannot be produced by artificial means. As you are aware, to bring about unity in their ranks has always been a major problem for all human societies.

Let me give a few illustrative examples before trying to explain what the real springhead of unity and solidarity is. These examples come from the life of the Prophet, peace be upon him.

Abū 'Azīz bin 'Umair was one of the unbelievers of Makka, taken prisoner at the Battle of Badr. His brother, Muṣ'ab bin 'Umair was a Muslim who had migrated to Madina and was the standard-bearer of the Islamic forces. When Abū 'Azīz was being bound, Muṣ'ab told the man doing it to tie hard and true as this was a rich man and would bring a good ransom. Upon this, Abū 'Azīz exclaimed: 'Brother! I had expected that you would put in a kind word on my behalf and tell him to tie my hands gently as I was your own brother, but you are telling him to bind firmly so that a large sum of money may be realised from me for my liberation'. Muṣ'ab bin 'Umair's reply will always be remembered in the annals of moral and spiritual revolutions.

He observed, 'You are not my brother, rather he that is tying your hands'.

Unity based on faith and loftiness of shared purpose had brought about such a transformation in the life of Muṣ'ab bin 'Umair, and to such a pitch, that he could bluntly tell his brother: 'One who is tying your hands is my brother and not you, because a new bond has sprung up between us which, though it has nothing to do with blood, is much more precious than the ties of kinship and lineage'.

The second incident is recounted by a Companion of the Prophet, peace be upon him, Abū Jahm bin Ḥudhaifa. He relates — 'Once, during the Battle of Yarmūk, I went into the battlefield in search of my cousin. I knew that those wounded in a battle are tormented by thirst, and so I was carrying a small water-bag with me thinking that he might be in his dying moments and I would pour some water in his mouth and wash his face. When I reached my cousin, I found that he was in the pangs of death, his lips parched. I offered him a cup of water but, at that moment, a groan was heard and my cousin said, 'This brother of mine is in greater need of water. Give the cup to him and leave me to my fate'. So, I went to him and as I was offering him the drink, the groan of another man was heard upon which he requested me to give the water to that man. It went on like that and when I carried the cup to one wounded person, he pointed towards another till I returned to my cousin and saw that he had breathed his last. I, thereupon, went to the second man, and then to the third man and so on, only to find that they too were dead. My cup remained untouched, and those noble-hearted servants went to meet their Maker without taking a sip from it'.

The third incident is still more remarkable. In the very thick of the Battle of Yarmūk, the Caliph 'Umar decided to relieve his general, Khālid bin Walīd, of the command of the Islamic forces, and appoint Abū 'Ubaida in his place. General Khālid had become a legendary figure around whom the myth of invincibility had grown up on account of his glorious exploits in war. This was, perhaps, why 'Umar wanted to replace him: he wanted to discourage the impression that Khālid and victory went together, because people had begun to rely upon him for overcoming the enemy instead of upon God. When the order for Khālid's removal came, preparations were being mounted for a decisive attack and the Caliph 'Umar had ordered that the headgear of General Khālid should be taken off and wound around his neck so that people knew that he had been dismissed. The general showed not a trace of sorrow or anger when the order was communicated to him. With unbelievable calmness he said: 'I believe and I submit. There will be no change in my conduct. If I was fighting for God, I shall still fight, and if I was fighting for 'Umar, I have every right to withdraw for he has expressed lack of faith in me and deprived me of such an honour'. He continued to fight with his usual skill and bravery. The dismissal made no difference to his determination and enthusiasm. In the so-called progressive societies of the present time if a person is relieved of his office he is affected with heart burning and becomes sulky and glum.

Unity of faith, unity of cause and unity of love can bring about marvellous results, provided that the faith, the cause or the love, is all-pervading. It is a great folly to think that mere agreement upon an aim is sufficient. One should be in love with it. Incidents such as I have just described take place when those who strive for their cause become like moths around a candle.

But some of you may say: The incidents you recall belong to the golden age of Islam, the age of the Blessed Prophet, and his Companions, when hearts had been purged of sin and immorality:

> But Allah hath endeared the faith to you and hath beautified it in your hearts, and hath made disbelief and lewdness and rebellion hateful unto you. (*al-Ḥujurāt,* 49: 7)

And you may ask: Have, since that age, examples of a like virtue occurred that may more readily inspire us now, in the twentieth century, so far away from the times of the Prophet?, peace be upon him.

I say that such remarkable examples of unity and sacrifice have recurred and will recur if the hold on faith is firm and commitment absolute, and if there is a reformer who can dye everyone in the colour of the same zeal and devotion.

147

For the moment, let me recall two incidents that took place in the course of the struggle launched by Syed Ahmad Shahīd (martyred 6 May, 1831) for the revival of Islam. Not so much time has passed since then and, what is more, these incidents belong to the days when the British had a firm hold in India and Muslim society had fallen considerably under the influence of Western civilisation.

Mawlavī Abdul Wahhāb of Lucknow was in charge of the distribution of grain and flour at Panjtar, the headquarters of Syed Shahīd's army of *Mujāhidīn*. While distributing the flour, he recited the Qur'ān, and sometimes would give the quota of twenty or twenty-five persons to one man without weighing, yet no-one got more or less than his allotted share.

One day, as he was distributing the flour, Mīr Imām 'Alī 'Azīmābādī came for his daily allowance. The flour was being dealt out by turn to the *Mujāhidīn,* and the Mīr was in a hurry. He was a powerfully-built man and wanted to be served before those who had come earlier. Mawlavī Abdul Wahhāb told him to await his turn, but he would not listen and pushed Mawlavī Abdul Wahhāb so hard that he fell down. Some Qandhārīs were also sitting there, waiting for their turn. They were annoyed at the behaviour of Mīr Imām 'Alī and rushed at him. But Mawlavī Abdul Wahhāb checked them, saying 'He is my brother. If he pushed, he pushed me. What have you to do with it?' The incident was reported to Syed Shahīd and when Mawlavī Abdul Wahhāb went to see him in the evening, he enquired from him about what Mīr Imām 'Alī had done. 'As far as I am concerned', replied Abdul Wahhāb, 'he did nothing. He is a very good man. He had come for his allowance of flour but it was not his turn, and he did not like to wait. In the meantime, he collided against me. That was all'. When Mīr Imām 'Alī came to know of what Abdul Wahhāb had said about him, he felt deeply ashamed and apologised to him and embraced him in Syed Shahīd's presence.

A more inspiring incident which reminds one of the earliest decades of Islam is that of Lahori who, also, was a member of the glorious band of *Mujāhidīn* who had gathered around Syed Ahmad Shahīd.

It is related that once Lahori, a very simple-minded man

148

who, jointly with Shaikh Ināyatullāh, looked after the preparation of fodder for the horses, got angry with his colleague. Ināyatullāh (a man very close to Syed Shahīd) lost his temper and, in the altercation that followed, delivered such a blow on Lahori's head that he dropped to the ground groaning. When Syed Shahīd heard about it, he reproved Shaikh Ināyatullāh severely and said, 'You may have thought that you were an old colleague of mine and slept near my bed — quite forgetting that we came here to serve God's cause — and therefore you do such shameful things. You thought that Lahori was the groom of Qazi Madani and a very poor and ugly-looking person, and you hit him for that reason. You have done a great wrong. With me, you and Lahori are alike. No one has superiority over the other. We are all here to serve the cause of God'.

After this, Syed Shahīd had Lahori and Ināyatullāh taken to the *Qāḍi* (judge) with orders that the matter be decided according to the *Sharī'ah* and no leniency shown.

On the next day, in the forenoon, Lahori and Ināyatullāh were brought before the *Qāḍī* who made them sit before him, and, turning first to Ināyatullāh, rebuked him sternly, saying that he had done a great wrong for which he deserved to be punished. Then, addressing Lahori, the *Qāḍī* remarked, 'Brother, you are a very good and well-intentioned person. You all have left your homes in India and come to this distant place solely for waging war in the way of God so that He may be pleased with you and reward you in the Hereafter. As for this world, it is a temporary one. Ināyatullāh is your brother though he has assaulted you out of the misfortune of his bad temper. If you forgive him, it will be very good and God will reward you for it in the Hereafter, and if you take revenge, you will be within your rights but you will not get the reward that is promised on forgiving. To forgive is the desire of God and the Messenger, and so it is allowed to take a just revenge. But in forgiving there is a reward and in taking revenge only the satisfaction of the self.'

On hearing this, Lahori said, 'Honourable *Qāḍī*! I will get the reward if I forgive Ināyatullāh, and if I avenge myself, we will be quits; but will there be any sin in it?' 'There will be no sin', replied the *Qāḍī*. 'Both are prescribed by God and the Messenger. Choose whichever you like'. 'Then I demand my right' said Lahori. After a pause, the *Qāḍī* observed 'Brother Lahori, your right is that you hit Ināyatullāh at the same place where he hit you'. He made Ināyatullāh stand before Lahori and told the latter to take his revenge. 'My right is that I strike him twice at that very place. Is it not?' asked Lahori. 'Of course', the *Qāḍī* replied.

Those who were witnessing the trial were filled with consternation; they felt sure that Lahori would not let Ināyatullāh go without having his revenge. But Lahori had other ideas. He said, 'Well, brothers, you are a witness to the fact that the *Qāḍī* has upheld my claim. I can take the revenge. But I forego it for the good pleasure of the Lord'. He then embraced Ināyatullāh and shook hands with him. With one voice, everyone complimented Lahori and said that he had done what only a truly devout and godly man could do.

No-one can attain such moral stature without a genuine love for God and the Messenger, peace be upon him, and that love cannot be produced simply by study and reflection nor by listening to speeches. I appreciate what has been said here in papers and speeches, but on careful thought, you will surely agree that this is not the way that love is generated. A profound study of the life, sayings and acts of the Prophet, peace be upon him, is essential for generating the sentiment of devotion and self-abnegation; not a formal study, but one reaching deep into one's moral and spiritual nature.

The honour you have done me, the affection and trust you have shown, as well as the long journey I have undertaken to be with you, demand that I put at your disposal all that I have of substance from my knowledge and experience. Therefore I put it to you that there is nothing more precious, dynamic and inspiring, in the vast treasure-house of Islam than the Qur'ān and the life of the Prophet, peace be upon him. The Book of God, the Qur'ān, is something we can honestly be proud of. It is the greatest fountain-head of strength and vitality through which we can win hearts, check the selfish propensities of the ego and control the appetites of the flesh. The Qur'ān can transform our lives and lift us from the lowness of the earth to the height of the skies. The power and energy that sprang from it in the earliest decades of Islam have not dried up. Next in importance is the life of the Prophet, peace be upon him. I appeal to you most fervently to develop the strongest attachment for the Qur'ān, and then for the life-story of the Prophet, peace be upon him. This may bring about a revolution in the lives of men and give rise to a new *Ummah,* a new community.

Self-indulgence, self-worship and self-seeking have always been the bane of the Muslims. We have never been humbled by our enemies alone. It is on account of our own internal strifes and dissensions that we have suffered defeats and lost lands. Take the case of Spain. The largest single factor leading to the eviction of Islam from that land was our internecine quarrels. I refuse to believe that it was the might of Christianity alone that forced the Muslims out of Spain. No mean part was played by the mutual rivalries of the Northern Arabs, the Yemenite Arabs and the Hijazis that had been rife for a long time. It was the suicidal wars among them and the Rabī'a and the Mudar, that culminated in the expulsion of Islam, and, Spain, in the words of Iqbal, was deprived of the *adhān,* the call to Prayer:

Thy land is like the heavens in the sight of the stars,
For ages, alas, thy atmosphere has remained bereft of *adhān.*

The same story has been repeated in most of the Islamic countries. In India too, the downfall of the Mughal rule was brought about, mainly, by domestic feuds and factions and intrigues and uprisings.

The malady of self-seeking and earthly-mindedness cannot be overcome only by sermons and seminars. To subdue anything you have to use an agent more powerful than it. If we have to put out fire, we pour water on it, and for softening iron, we use fire. Selfishness and self-worship cannot be wished away, and unity and brotherly love are not engendered by public discourses and pious declarations.

When personal, tribal or factional interests are given preference over the aims and interests of Islam, it will lead to the same disastrous results that have overtaken the Indian Muslims.

When in Europe, I said, again and again, to my Muslim brothers there: 'You are faced with a tremendous challenge. On the day of Judgement, the Lord will call you to account and the Blessed Prophet, will enquire: We had given you a very large field in which you could raise the banner of Islamic renaissance and give the call of Faith and conquer the conquerors of the world, but you started rushing at each other's throats and got involved in mutually destructive struggles for power. Now, what answer will you give?'

The springhead of love, brothers, is in the heart. Mutual affection, sympathy and fellow-feeling cannot be produced by external means and without the love of God, and the love of God is generated by offering *Ṣalāt,* shedding tears, making earnest entreaties to Him, and praying in the silent hours of the night for elevation in the ranks of believing brethren:

> 'Our Lord! Forgive us and our brethren who were before us in the faith and place not in our hearts any rancour towards those who believe. Our Lord! Thou art full of Pity, Merciful.' (*al-Ḥashr,* 59: 10)

People can forgive even their bitterest enemies. I will tell you of an incident. Once a person suspected a very saintly man of stealing his purse, and without any proof or enquiry, started beating him severely. Other people intervened and scolded him for his meanness. The man realised his mistake and apologised to the man. The godly man then said, 'Brother, there is no question of an apology. When you were beating me, I was beseeching the Lord "Oh God! If Thou hast decided that I enter Paradise then I will not set foot in it until Thou allowest this man, also, who is beating me, to enter with me". I was making this Prayer. Why speak of my having a grievance against you?'

Keep such examples before you. You will find many in the lives of the Prophet, peace be upon him, and his Companions. Go back from here with the resolve that you will make the life of the Prophet, peace be upon him, your constant companion and seek guidance from it. Also, read as much as possible, about the life and character of the blessed Companions. Improve your Prayer.

We are the bondsmen of the Lord. If we do not set right

our bond with God, and our hearts are not imbued with love for Him, we can never feel sincerely for His creatures, nor be truly high-minded and self-sacrificing, for the mainspring of all these qualities and emotions, in Islam, is the love of God and the Prophet, peace be upon him.

Chapter Thirteen

Protect your Faith and your Heritage

If faith is the only key to life in Islam, one would want to know the ways of protecting and strengthening faith. This is what Nadwi sets out here:

Firstly, give precedence to Islam over every other thing and in all circumstances. Neither wealth nor status should become more important. Even be prepared to migrate back, to your country of origin, if you find it difficult to preserve your faith.

Secondly, let all your actions be with the sole intention of seeking the pleasure of your Creator. Running after the world may lead nowhere; living for your Lord alone may give worldly benefits as well. The intention also includes a conscious desire to reap the rewards promised by Allah and His Messenger.

Thirdly, continuously take account of your own intentions and deeds.

Fourthly, maintain links with the religious environment in the countries of your origin. This will recharge the dried up sensitivities and emotions within you.

Fifthly, though recently produced Islamic literature is important, beware of the folly of ignoring or underrating, or denegrating the tremendous contributions made by the earlier generations. It is very important to preserve an attitude of respect and recognition to them.

Sixthly, he asks that you hold fast to Prayers, both obligatory and voluntary.

Finally, he warns against emulating the ways of the Western culture, especially in matters like the intermingling of sexes. [Ed.]

13

I have been travelling through the United States and Canada for the last three weeks and have, during that time, made dozens of speeches in Urdu and Arabic. But a speech is after all a formal public address with some well-worked rhetorical flourishes to hammer home certain ideas. Brother and sister Muslims and friends, I should like to speak informally, as one of the family. I shall recount some personal impressions and offer a few suggestions, all in the earnest hope that you will think them over seriously.

After meeting different people and representatives of different organisations, I have arrived at certain conclusions. These are, so to speak, the pluses I have taken during this visit for which I am deeply grateful to MSA and other well-wishers. I pray to God, and ask you also to join me in the prayer, that at today's meeting, I may say only what is going to be useful and beneficial to you in the long run, and that this journey of mine does not turn out to be a futile exercise. For I am often assailed by doubt about whether I have justified all the trouble — it has been a long and expensive affair and friends have spared no pains to make it possible. Will I not be called by God to account for it? Maybe I have committed errors during the trip and failed to live up to expectations. May what I am going to say today serve to make up for my failings.

There is no dearth of speeches, and it has, also, become customary to put questions to the speaker at the end of a speech. Often it happens that even during a speech the listeners begin to formulate questions in their minds. In the midst of it all, however, the real thing being said is forgotten. I hope you will not indulge in this exercise until I have

---

From a speech delivered at the Muslim Community Centre of Chicago on 20 June, 1977. As there was a very representative gathering and it was going to be the last speech of the tour, Nadwi thought it fit to restate briefly what he had seen and felt during his stay in that part of the world, and also to offer some suggestions.

finished.

GUARD AND STRENGTHEN YOUR FAITH

First of all, let me implore you to guard the wealth that you possess in Islam. Do not lose it at any cost. If you fully realised how short the life of the world has been and how long is the life that is to come and through what stages you are to pass in the Hereafter, your hair would stand on end in awe. Who will be more unfortunate than ourselves if we have done everything here in America but have allowed to waste the provision of the fear of God and solicitude for the Hereafter. I swear by God that it would have been much better to starve than to invite the risk and imperil the religious future of our children. We will be the greatest losers if we gain everything but lose the wealth of faith.

The Messenger of God, peace be upon him, said, 'One of the three qualities essential for tasting the sweetness of faith is that the idea of going back to apostasy after a man has embraced Islam is as dreadful to him as being thrown into fire'.

Let us not, by our conduct, be the verifiers of the truth of these verses of the Qur'ān:

> Shall We tell you of those who lose most in respect of their deeds? Those whose efforts have been wasted in this life, while they thought they were acquiring good by their works. (*al-Kahf,* 18: 103-4)

The poor souls believed that they were acquiring good through their works. What I fear is that this might be applicable to us. Many people do realise when they are doing something reprehensible or immoral. But a peculiar curse of this modern civilisation is that it never occurs to a man that he can err. He is so smug and self-satisfied. For instance, if one enquires from anyone in India or Pakistan where his brother is and what he is doing, he will reply with a twinkle in his eye, *Māshā' Allāh,* he is in America and earning so many thousand dollars'. This is what is being said back home. Here, for our part, we hear — 'How well we have done. What would we be earning had we stayed in Hyderabad, Uttar Pradesh, Bihar, Lahore or Karachi? Here we are getting more

157

than what a Governor or Minister in India or Pakistan gets'.

Be on your guard against this frame of mind and choose the security and preservation of Faith above every kind of worldly success so that you do not depart from this world save as truthful Muslims. I say that a man who lives in America and takes the Faith unimpaired with him to the next world will, perhaps, merit a greater reward than he who dies in Arabia because he protects the lamp of his faith against all sorts of storms and tempests. It is related that the Prophet of God, peace be upon him, said:

> 'Some of my brothers will be steadfast in Faith and observe their duty to God'. 'Are we not your brothers?' asked the Companions. 'You are my Companions', replied the Prophet, 'but my brothers are those who have not seen me. They will be born much later and their faith will be on the unseen, i.e. they will embrace Islam without seeing me'.

Believe me, you can attain the highest level of spiritual excellence in America and the good work you do here will be infinitely more pleasing to the Lord — just as the mother feels the more strongly for her child when it is far off and prays the more earnestly for its safety. You are the children of Islam who are placed far away from its cradle and surrounded by forces of apostasy and materialism. You will, therefore, be receiving the special attention of God. Do not despair of His mercy.

First, and above all, give precedence to Islam in every circumstance. Poverty with faith is a million times better than power and wealth without it. By the grace of God, you are an intelligent and educated people. Should there be the least danger to faith go back to your native land or to any other place where there is the security of faith; go, and take your family, go even if you have to go on foot. Whatever the conditions, your endeavour should be to live up to the Divine commandment: 'And die not save as men who have surrendered (unto Him)' (al-Baqara, 2: 132).

PURIFY YOUR INTENTION

Secondly, let all your deeds be intended in order to seek the favour and countenance of God — no other consideration, whether of fortune or position, should prevail. Worldly gain will, *Inshā' Allāh,* come your way according to your ability and application, but take care of your intention so that you may receive the due reward on what you do. As a Tradition of the Prophet, peace be upon him, reads:

> 'The actions are judged according to intentions, and to every man is due what he intended. Thus, whosoever migrates for the sake of Allah and His Apostle, his migration is accounted for the sake of Allah and His Apostle; and whosoever migrates for the sake of this world or to wed a woman, it will be accounted only for the purpose for which it is intended'

Look into your intention from time to time, and make it right. The aim and idea behind all your acts should be the pleasure and favour of God and the service of Islam and Muslims. You will, then, *Inshā' Allāh,* earn the reward equal in value to that on *Jihād,* and sometimes, even on martyrdom.

Your effort should be to do everything with *īmān* (faith in God) and *ihtisāb* (confident expectation of Divine recompense). A deed carries weight with God only when it is performed with *īmān* and *ihtisāb.* For example, it is stated in a Tradition about the Fasts of Ramaḍān that 'whoever keeps the fasts of Ramaḍān with *īmān* and *ihtisāb,* all his previous sins will be forgiven'.

You may well ask how can fasting be observed with *bad-niyyatī* (bad intention). Brothers, *bad-niyyatī* is one thing; *be-niyyatī* (absence of intention) is another; and, as I often say, Muslims are more a victim of *be-niyyatī* than *bad-niyyatī.* At the time of performing a deed they care not to ask themselves whether they are doing it with the intention of pleasing God or out of mere habit and custom or some other motive.

LOOK AFTER THE INWARD

Thirdly, do not be self-complacent. Look inward, into your own heart and mind. Keep your deeds under constant review by cultivating the habit of self-criticism, by being your own examiner.

KEEP CONTACT WITH ISLAMIC ENVIRONMENT

Fourthly, I would advise you to visit your native countries regularly, every two years or so. Maintain a living contact with the places of your origin. It would be better if you could go to India, Pakistan or the cities of Makka and Madina and spend some time there in a religious environment and in the company of virtuous and godly men. The wells of religious fervour and God-consciousness will dry up within you if you go on living here without a break. The battery of the heart must be recharged from time to time by going to your country and spending a few months there. I have noticed that there is a marked difference between those who maintain contact with their native lands and those who do not. People who are out of touch with their home countries generally develop an insensitiveness towards religious feelings, values and ideals.

Even if they offer Prayer and observe fasting, it is in a routine, almost off-hand manner. I accept that this, too, is not unavailing, but they grow indifferent to the spiritual content of these acts. They fail to appreciate their substance and have no real idea of the state of the willing bondsmen of the Lord, of the quality of their Prayers and the depth and intensity of their feelings.

Religious environment is in the nature of a powerhouse. By the grace of God, this environment still exists in India and Pakistan and men of high moral and spiritual stature are found in whose company the grime and rust of impoverished belief is removed from the heart. I say this from personal experience. I have felt this even in Saudi Arabia which I visit frequently. There too I have observed that families who have remained in contact with India are in much better shape than those who have adopted the Arab culture and servered their ties with India.

Makka and Madina are, of course, the real centres of Islam, but they too have started accepting thoughtlessly the influence of the Western civilisation and the petro-dollars are playing havoc with the social and cultural values of the Arabs. What is more, a sort of complacency is created when people take up residence in those blessed cities. 'We are the inhabitants of Hijaz, we live under the shadow of the House of God, Ka'ba' — this is how they begin to feel.

160

On the contrary, it is the religious condition of those who maintain a living contact with India that is better and more secure: they make regular return visits, do not lose touch with Urdu in which so many religious books and magazines are published, and welcome the theologians and spiritual mentors from India and Pakistan as their guests and learn from them the laws and principles of the *Sharī'ah;* they go more frequently to Makka and Madina, perform the *'umra* more often and have a greater attachment to the holy city of Madina.

DO NOT LOOK DOWN UPON YOUR PRECIOUS HERITAGE

Fifthly, I notice that you, living here in America, have a great interest in Islamic literature. There is a growing demand in the United States and Canada for good religious books in English and Urdu, and theologians, writers and leaders from Islamic countries come here and meetings are arranged in their honour. Now, let me impress upon you not to deprecate nor think ill of those who in past times have served the cause of faith.

It is a most dangerous trend and a grave folly. Those of our brothers whose knowledge is derived solely from books are, generally, the most prone to this attitude. When they read such articles or books as are now available they jump to the conclusion that no one had hitherto undertaken a thorough study of Islam. In their immaturity they invent criteria for measuring service to faith, and proceed to pronounce judgement on every reformer of past times. But I tell you they have no idea of the difficult circumstances in which these deep-hearted men carried out their mission. I can only pity the man who, for instance, criticises Shaikh 'Abdul Qādir Jīlānī for spending all his time giving sermons and caring nothing for the setting up of an Islamic state, even though in his days the Abbasid Caliph had suspended the Islamic order.

Do you not know of the magnificent work done by this illustrious man of God? Africa is still indebted to him, for it was through his Order that Islam spread there, and also in India, Indonesia and many other countries. God alone knows how many dead hearts were brought to life by him and how many men were delivered from apostasy and polytheism to Islam through his efforts.

He knew that the Abbasid Caliphs belonged to the family of the Blessed Prophet; they were Arabs and Hashimites, and understood the Qur'ān as well as he did. Then, why did they not acquit themselves in a manner befitting Caliphs of Islam? He was convinced that at the root of their failure lay an excessive fondness for power and wealth. So, he set himself first to the task of the moral and spiritual regeneration of the society as a whole. Ask yourselves what is wrong with Pakistan? Are not that country and its rulers Muslims? Was it not created in the name of Islam? Only the other day a Pakistani friend was telling me how a young man, related to him, had joined a procession at Lyallpur to protest against the Government. Someone in the procession raised the cry, 'On what was the foundation of Pakistan laid?' The young man replied, 'On *Lā ilāha illāllāh Muḥammadur Rasūlullāh'*. He had hardly finished the sentence when a bullet hit him in the chest and he dropped to the ground dead.[1] Now, tell me, was that shot fired by a Muslim or a non-Muslim? Why does this happen? Why does a Muslim kill a Muslim? If a person sincerely believed that his country's malaise was due primarily to headlong involvement in worldly aims and pleasures and he spent his life fighting against it, what was wrong with that?

Sometimes, it is imagined that if a Muslim is not working for the establishment of an Islamic state, he is simply wasting his time and achieving nothing, no matter if he is a Shaikh 'Abdul Qādir Jīlānī or Mujaddid Al-Thānī or Shāh Walīullāh. This view is the effect of an imperfect reading of history. I say without hesitation that if Islam is safe and alive in the world, today, the credit for it does not go to any one section of the *Ummah*. The theologians, the jurists, the scholars of the Traditions, the religious teachers, the spiritual mentors and the Sufi saints, they have all played their part.

It may be argued that Imām Abū Ḥanīfa only taught the rules and proprieties of Prayer and fasting while he should

---

1 It should be noted that the incident took place in the days of Mr. Zulfikar Ali Bhutto, after the last general elections.

have seized power and established an Islamic state. But if, my friends, the Islamic state had come into being, who would have been there to teach how Prayer was to be offered? And of what worth is a Caliphate in which no one knows how to perform Prayer?

> Those who, if We give them power in the land, establish worship and pay the poor due and enjoin what is right and forbid iniquity. And Allah's is the sequel of events. (*al-Ḥajj*, 22: 41)

The Qur'ān does not say that those whom We will teach how to offer Prayer will establish the Islamic Government, but that power and rule is meant for paving the way for Prayer so that there should remain no excuse for neglect. Says the Lord: 'Until persecution is no more, and religion is all for Allah'. (*al-Anfāl*, 8: 39)

Never think that those who preceded us were worthless men, who did not understand Islam or who did not try to establish the whole of it, in form as well as in spirit. In fact, they were all doing their best to serve the cause of Islam: some were giving sermons, some teaching the Traditions, others issuing religious decrees and still others writing books. According to his aptitude and circumstances, each of those predecessors was engaged in the propagation and preservation of Islam and in the moral and spiritual instruction of Muslims.

We must not denigrate those who dedicated their lives to teaching the name of Allah, to training and inspiring the Muslims. It would be the height of ingratitude to deny or depreciate the services to Islam of those men, generally known by the name of Sufis. Do you not know what a glorious role the Sufis have played? They have saved the Islamic society from debasement and degeneration. This is a fact. The tide of materialism would have swept the Muslim *Millah* away like a straw had they not performed the fundamental duty. It was their work that prevented sensuality and self-indulgence from becoming the order of the day among Muslims: when anyone succumbed to the temptations of Satan or to his own baser instincts, he went to those godly men and repented. The Sufi saints and spiritual mentors

163

produced the right kind of men and took from each the work for which he was most suited. Our reading history is sometime defective. As I have argued in the Foreword of *Tārīkh-i-Da'wat-o-'Azīmat*,[2] the defect lies not in the history itself, but in the presentation of it as a story revolving round the courts of kings and noble lords, without any worthwhile study of the endeavours to reform and renovate. Take away this imbalance in presentation, and no empty deserts, no failures of will and spirit, will appear in the history of our society.

Do not be misled into believing that it is only now that some individuals have begun to understand Islam, that no-one had achieved this earlier. For one thing, to do this puts Islam in a very poor light. The continuance of the Qur'ān will become doubtful and so too its clarity and accessibility which have been made manifest in Divine utterances, such as 'By the Scripture which maketh plain' (*al-Zukhruf*, 43: 2), and 'This is clear Arabic speech' (*al-Naḥl*, 16: 103).

Moreover, how can we be sure that the book which no-one could understand for twelve hundred years has now been completely understood? For my part, I regard as harmful any book or article that gives the impression that the meaning of Islam has not been fully grasped during all these twelve hundred years or that some of the Islamic truths are yet to be unravelled. I can never accept it. The fundamental doctrines of Islam, the Qur'ānic truths and the imperatives of faith have always been with us, without interruption, and whoever imagines that these have not been understood for a long time, betrays a lamentable lack of vision. I challenge anyone to prove that any Islamic truth has been forgotten at any one time by the whole of the Islamic world. Ibn Taymiyyah has gone to the extent of claiming that there is not even one *Sunnah*[3] which might have been forsaken by the Muslims as a whole. If it had gone unobserved in one part of the Muslim world, it was yet alive in another part.

---

2 By the present author, brought out in English as *Saviours of the Islamic Spirit*.

3 An authenticated practice of the Holy Prophet, peace be upon him, an example set by him.

Men of faith live in the world like the sun,
Setting here, rising there; rising here, setting there.

The realities of Islam do not become altogether extinct. If they fade away at one place, men arise at another place to stake their lives for the survival of those truths. Never imagine that no-one has been able to understand Islam properly though it has been with us for over a thousand years, as if it were something of a riddle or enigma. It is not like the Christian doctrine of the Trinity which needs an army of explicators to make sense of it — it is nothing of this sort.

We may not meet again, and, hence, my eagerness to bring the point home to you. I do not want to blame or criticise anyone. My object simply is that the whole thing become clear in your minds.

So, have a good opinion of our God-fearing precursors and pray for them. It is set forth in the Qur'ān:

> And those who come (into the faith) after them and pray: Our Lord! Forgive us and our brethren who were before us in the faith and place not in our hearts any rancour towards those who believe. Our Lord! Thou art Full of Pity, Merciful. (al-Ḥashr, 59: 10)

There is a great protection for faith in thinking well of the precursors, otherwise when the tongue becomes impudent its impudence may keep no bounds.

My brothers, can we dare to say that they did not understand the faith who were much better than us in knowledge, action and repentance? If they did not understand, how can we be sure that we do?

PERFORM PRAYERS

Sixthly, performing Prayer, also helps greatly in the protection of faith. Do your best to offer Prayer regularly and at the correct times. As the Caliph 'Umar said 'The most important in all your activities and affairs is Prayer. He who protects it, will protect everything, and he who neglects it, will not let anything remain'. Hold fast to Prayer; do not neglect it wherever you are. If nothing more, offer at least the *fard*[4] part, but it is desirable to offer the *sunnahs*[5] and *nawāfil*[6] as well, for they act as a shield for the obligatory *(fard)*.

BEWARE OF WESTERN CIVILISATION

Beware, finally, of the Western civilisation which is now at the peak of its glory and declining. I have noticed here a great laxity in some matters. To put it plainly, the intermixing of the sexes has attained alarming proportions. Do your best to avoid mixed gatherings. If it is necessary for you to attend a party or meeting where ladies are present, maintain a respectful posture. At such gatherings there should be a separate enclosure, even a separate passageway, for men and women. There is a great protection in it. The Islamic social and cultural design is based on very wise principles and sound and healthy considerations. Free intercourse between men and women is strictly forbidden in Islam, so do not accept such influences of American civilisation. As far as possible, protect the Islamic culture and civilisation: think through its distinctive qualities and standards and try to preserve them.

Please do not misunderstand me. I am not advocating cultural arrogance, nor do I support a hostile or negative attitude towards anyone. Whatever I have said is in a spirit of sincerity and well-wishing. I entertain respect for everyone and seek a generous, broad temperament. I have relations with people belonging to different schools of thought and hold them in esteem. It is out of a feeling of moral obligation that I have drawn your attention to these things.

I shall, *Inshā' Allāh,* be praying for you and hope that you too will remember me in your Prayers.

---

4 i.e. obligatory Prayers.
5 & 6 i.e. optional Prayers but sanctified by the practice of the Holy Prophet, peace be upon him.

Chapter Fourteen

The Role of Muslim Women

Responsibilities that devolve upon Muslims in the West must be shared equally by men and women. The nature and degree of the responsibility of women is neither less nor different from that of men, though their functions may be separate. All that Nadwi has so far said applies equally to both. However, here, he makes a separate appeal to women, more appropriate to their role and circumstances.

Man and woman are totally interdependent, he says. Their relationship, mutual rights and obligations are rooted in Divine guidance. The relationship between the two, established in the name of Allah, is unique. It is not a necessity, but an act of worship.

Women must also come forward to convey the message of Islam to the Western people. [Ed.]

14

Brothers and sisters, I am deeply indebted to you for giving me this opportunity to express my views on a question so fundamental to social and personal relations. Let me begin by reciting a verse of the Qur'ān and then try to explain the Islamic viewpoint on social relations, and indicate how realistic it is in its approach. The verse is from *Sūra al-Nisā'*, (its very title should be enough to show what place Islam gives to women). It reads:

> O Mankind! Be careful of your duty to your Lord Who created you from a single soul and from it created its mate and from these two has spread abroad a multitude of men and women. Be careful of your duty towards Allah through Whom you demand your mutual (rights), and towards the wombs (that bore you).
> Lo! Allah has been a Watcher over you. (4: 1)

I believe this verse expresses simply and forcefully the Islamic standpoint on the status of women and the mutual rights and duties of the two sexes. First of all, God makes it clear that both men and women have been created in the same manner and their destinies are inter-related, as if they are the two parts of a single body. The little biological divergence is for no other reason than that they perform the journey of life comfortably.

Both male and female have been created of a single soul, and, then, that single soul was moulded into two shapes, but there is no conflict or hostility between them. In life's journey, man has been provided with a partner from his own species and who is a part of his body. The human race originates from this pair. God blessed their union, love and companionship with great abundance so that those who were originally two multiplied into millions till no one can tell how

From a speech delivered at a seminar for Muslim women in Chicago on 19 June, 1977.

many have been born into the world. The number is known only to God: He has alluded to their abundance by using the word 'multitude'.

The Lord, then, says: *'Fear Allah in Whose Name you lay your claim on one another'.* The revolutionary idea that in human affairs, no one is sufficient unto himself was propounded for the first time by the Qur'ān. All men are dependent on one another. Everyone is at once the receiver and the giver; not that the receivers are on one side and the givers on the opposite. Everyone is linked in the mesh of rights and duties; in the network of civilised life each stands in need of others.

Without a woman, no man can accomplish his natural journey in a pleasant and comfortable manner, and, in the same way, no virtuous woman can lead a happy and contented life without a life-partner. The Creator has made them dependent on each other so that without one another the life of each must remain incomplete.

Again, it is proclaimed that it is Allah in whose name you should demand your rights of one another. The Islamic society is founded upon belief in God, in His power, majesty and Oneness. The partnership between a Muslim man and a Muslim woman becomes legitimate in the name of Allah. It is the name of Allah that makes strangers kindred, and distant ones near ones.

The bond between man and wife is a bond of faith and love, and in its depth, intimacy and naturalness, it is absolutely unique. All this is the miracle of the name of Allah. A new world is born by invoking His name. A Muslim man and a Muslim woman cannot mix freely with one another; sometimes, they cannot even travel together; until the name of Allah comes to dwell between them and the sacred tie is forged.

The Qur'ān, in its inimitable style, has represented the basic reality of human society, the interdependence of its members, their co-relation and mutuality, in the few, simple words — 'through Whom ye demand your mutual rights'.

It, then, proceeds to urge upon us to be careful of our duty to Allah in whose name we make the unlawful lawful, and bring about a revolution in our lives. The Qur'ān has used another matchless expression, also, to describe the profound relationship between husband and wife. It says: 'They are raiment for you and ye are raiment for them' (*al-Baqara*, 2: 187). It is the Qur'ān alone that could use the word 'raiment' in this context. Clothing is essential for hiding nakedness and as an adornment of life. The parable conveys everything that can be said concerning the relationship of love, faith and trust between husband and wife. Just as without clothing a man looks more like an animal than a civilised being so, without a married life, he must be considered less than civilised.

In Islam matrimony is not regarded as a necessity but given the status of an act of worship which brings a man closer to God. The concept of marriage is not based on biological or social necessity without which the enjoyment of life is not complete, but it is religious. The Blessed Prophet, furnished the greatest example of it in his own life. He said, 'The best among you is he who is good to his family, and, among you, I am the best for my family'. If you study the life of the Prophet, peace be upon him, you will be struck by instances of his respect for the fair sex and his regard for sentiments which are not to be found in the lives of the greatest champions of the rights of women, nor in the lives of the most illustrious holy men and law-givers, and not in the lives of the other Apostles. The pains the Blessed Prophet took to please his wives and make them happy, his sharing in their legitimate recreational activities, his careful impartial justice to them — these were of surpassing charm and nobleness.

With children also he was so kind and affectionate that he would even cut short Prayer, so dear to his heart, if he heard a child crying. It was the height of benevolence and sacrifice. Nothing could have been more precious to him than the Prayer. Yet, he would say, 'Sometimes, I like to prolong Prayer, but then I hear a child crying and shorten the service, thinking that its mother would be restless'.

These are the examples we have before us. The Lord exhorts us to protect the dignity of His name we have brought in, not merely using it to our advantage. This commandment is for both men and women. You are, now, living in American society. We have not only to introduce the tenets

170

of Islam to the American people but also to present before them living models of its family-system. Undoubtedly, Western civilisation is rapidly on the decline. One of the foremost causes of this is the disintegration of the family. Love and trust which are the cornerstone of married life are yielding to selfishness and sensuality. Modern philosophers are worried and studies are being undertaken for the preservation of the sanctity of the family. There ought to be love and sympathy on both sides for in that alone lies true happiness. Even poverty and starvation are tolerated with equanimity where there is love and the willingness to enter into and share the feelings of one another. There are, even now, many families in the East which do not have enough to eat and yet live happily because there is mutual love. Here, in the West there is everything — wealth, scientific innovation, and educational advancement — but many hearts are devoid of peace and contentment. They have not been able to turn their homes into a paradise. As Iqbal has said:

He sought the orbits of the stars, yet could not
Travel his own thought's world.

Modern man is equipped with power, but lacking in vision. The conqueror of solar radiation cannot brighten his own destiny; the seeker of the stars' orbits and, if Iqbal were alive today, he would have said, the traveller to the moon — cannot explore the world of his own ideas and make his home a place of bliss. He who had set out to turn the world into a paradise has ended up by making his own home a hell. Many Western homes are not blessed with peace and happiness. That is why they seek diversion in clubs and other out of home activities.

You are more aware of this distressing aspect of American life as you have been living here for as many as ten or twenty years, so I need not dwell upon it at length. The Qur'ānic verse I have quoted expounds the fundamental truth that human society is based upon interdependence and respect for each other's rights and needs. To realise this basic truth and to feel grateful to the person through whom the needs are fulfilled is an attitude of mind that Islam seeks to strengthen.

171

It requires everyone to consider himself linked to others and entertain respect for all members of the society.

May Allah guide you to the Straight Path and enable you to present the pattern of Islamic life and social conduct that will appeal to the Western people who have grown weary of life and encourage them to think over and examine closely the social commandments of Islam. In this way you can render a valuable service not only to this country but also to Islam. It is difficult, in the present circumstances, to think of a more positive and effective step towards the propagation of faith.

Chapter Fifteen

Cultural Serfdom and the
Role of Muslim Students

*Many students from Muslim countries come to the West
for higher education and stay here for long periods. They are
supposed eventually to return to their own countries. They
should play an effective role in spreading the message of
Islam in the West and preserve their identity while they are
here. At the same time they should be aware of the situation
in their countries of origin to which they will have to return
and know what role they must play there.*

*Towards this end, Nadwi first analyses the outcome of the
encounter between the West and the Muslim world in recent
years. While the nineteenth century saw one country after
another going under the yoke of foreign domination, the
twentieth century has witnessed their freedom from the
West's political domination. Is freedom real is another
question. What is obvious is that the intellectual, cultural and
moral subservience to Western civilisation remains as before,
rather the so-called political freedom has resulted in further
strengthening the cultural enslavement.*

*The Westernised élite who inherited power from the former
masters are in unremitting conflict, both politically and
culturally, with their own people in almost every Muslim
country. The masses believe in Islam and aspire for an Islamic
way of life. The rulers see matters entirely differently. Thus
the potential of the Muslim world is being wasted in internal
conflicts and tensions.*

*Unfortunately, laments Nadwi, the bright young men and
women leaving the gates of the Western institutes of learning
are remote and alien to the people to whom they are going*

back. They cannot speak a language which their people understand or a language which can penetrate their hearts. They are also unaware of the West's failure to create real 'men', or the dangers which technology poses.

Muslim students should, by all means, gain whatever useful knowledge they can, but they should also give to the West what it needs. [Ed.]

15

WESTERN DOMINANCE

Europe came into significant contact with the Islamic nations at the beginning of the nineteenth century. Only then, after its slow emergence from the medieval gloom and ignorance of the Dark Ages, was Europe able to reach out to the East. It is true that certain Western powers had made inroads into certain possessions of the Turks, but these were of minor significance. The real impact of Western civilisation was not really felt until one of the major Western powers attained a hold on India and Egypt — these, with Turkey, enjoyed eminence and authority not only in the Islamic East but in the entire world of that time.

India had pride of place — the populous Muslims there had wielded power for several hundred years with unparalleled pomp and glory; they had enriched different branches of Islamic learning and through intelligence and industry made their mark on the intellectual, political and social life of the country. But when, after the 1857 upheaval, the British government took over from the East India Company, it was thought that India would remain for ever under the British Crown. Egypt was of consequence because it became the intellectual centre of the Arab world: it boasted the great al-Azhar University, the work of whose scholars and theologians, poets and writers, was deeply admired all over the Islamic world. The importance of Turkey needs no explanation: it was the centre of Caliphate, the home of a capable, gallant and energetic people who played a crucial role in world history. When these three countries were introduced to the Western civilisation, they entered into a new world, their history took a new turn.

Whether by good or ill-fortune these three countries all fell within the sphere of British political influence at about the

---

From a speech given in the Union Hall of Leeds University, before a well-attended meeting of students from India and Pakistan, on Thursday, 26 June, 1969.

same time. The British government took direct control in India; it made Egypt a protectorate and imposed there a Political Agent under the excuse of facilitating repayment of British loans to Egypt. Turkey was able to stay free of domination by the West but it fell victim to the political machinations of the British. It might be said therefore that East and West crossed through the power-quest of Britain: the injury sustained by the East was likewise, as historians acknowledge, at the hands of this island nation. The East came to realise its economic backwardness as well as its military and political weakness through subjection to Britain.

INDEPENDENCE

But all this happened in the middle of the nineteenth century. In the more recent past, a tidal wave of national liberation emancipated, in quick succession, country after country from the political domination of the West. The era of foreign domination has come to an end, officially, as it had to, for it was unnatural. It was unnatural that one country should continue to govern the affairs of another fertile and populous land, from across the seven seas and against the will of the people inhabiting that land; this was a phenomenon lacking any inherent capacity for its own continuance. Had its continuance been further enforced it would, certainly by now have run its course. The British in this sense have proved themselves more realistic than the French — they were able to see the writing on the wall and 'granted' freedom to their subject nations.

Well, all Islamic countries have attained independence, India and Pakistan are tasting the fruits of freedom — you will say. But are they? What kind of independence is it where there remains intellectual, cultural, moral serfdom to Western civilisation? Those who have pondered the situation, studied it as it is, must see that freedom has in fact increased cultural bondage to the West, not removed it. Why so?

CULTURAL BONDAGE

Varied reasons have been advanced by different writers for this situation — I too have discussed the question at some length in one of my books on this subject.[1] For the present we need not go into the reasons — for the moment let us face the fact, and fact it certainly is, that political freedom has deepened cultural enslavement. No one, unless slavish and immature, could favour the political bondage of his country; yet, is it not true that ultimately cultural bondage is the deeper evil of the two?

Neither India nor Pakistan, nor those Arab countries still to achieve full freedom, have as yet realised what it means to be free. They have inherited the cultural and economic structures previously imposed upon them — and live within them. Such is their dependence upon the West that liberation has meant only a change of hands at upper level of government, without any change in the springhead supplying the vital impulse to run these governments. We draw on the West not only for knowledge in specific subjects or for specific skills but for the entire system of education. We ape the West in manners and modes of living. What is worse we even depend for our moral and religious precepts on researches done by Western scholars: even the Islamic sciences are judged from the standpoint evolved by Western educational institutions. Orientalists are held in high esteem even in the East, and it has been accepted everywhere that what they say is the last word and requires no further scrutiny. The insufferable weight upon every Islamic people of alien, crazy concepts, of values that have no grounding in, that even contradict, the principles of Islam and the demands of its own conscience — this insufferable weight is provoking everywhere a crisis of identity, a deep anxiety, a grave malaise — mental and spiritual.

RULERS AND THE RULED

There is unremitting conflict between the men in power, whose hopes and ambitions (albeit they are Muslims still) are modelled on the West, and the people they rule.

For the people are Muslim through and through: they believe in the Hereafter, in Paradise and Hell; they believe

---

1 *Western Civilisation — Islam and Muslims,* Academy of Islamic Research and Publications.

that they will have to render account for whatever they do in this life; they acknowledge that the life of this world, its pleasures and sorrows, is transitory; they are convinced that the ultimate end in view is preferable to immediate purely material objectives; that to eat, drink and be merry and have the fat of the land, is not the aim of life; they believe rather that the aim of life consists in being more humane, in living in awe of God, following the path of virtue and avoiding self-indulgence and sin, in observing the precepts of the Law revealed by God, in proper reverence for the teachings and example of the last Prophet of God, peace be upon him, in disseminating the message of peace and virtue to unbelieving humanity so that they too may learn and believe.

But the men in power have a quite different view of the world. They doubt the truths expressed by Islam. They doubt that there is a power behind what their senses reveal to them. They doubt that there is a life after death. They cannot believe that man can derive satisfaction and happiness from anything other than material assets and possessions. In consequence there is in the people they govern a growing unrest; the rulers have no commitment to the people's faith and so they waste their real energy, being unable to direct it to proper use.

Yet this energy is no slight thing. I told some Arab friends only yesterday that if our Eastern countries had a leadership properly aware of the inherent qualities of the people — of their strength, courage, enthusiasm, of their zeal and capacity for sacrifice, of their glorious past and present potentialities — there is no power on earth that could subdue them. This vigour and energy rests in the people's faith, in the power of that faith, a power to move mountains. Islam has still, for the people, the power to awaken their spirits to sacrifice — and they would sacrifice — their pleasures, their homes and possessions, even their lives, for the honour of God, of Islam and the Prophet of Islam, peace be upon him. No other cause could arouse in the people such enthusiasm, nor could that enthusiasm ever be subdued.

YOUTH AND THE WEST
But our bright young men and women leaving the gates of

Western universities seem out of touch with the strengths of their people, they do not know even themselves — perhaps it is these young men and women that are addressed in the couplet:

Get within yourself, and discover life's secret,
If you will not be mine, be true to yourself at least.

They return from the universities equipped with the knowledge of history and geography, individual psychology and mass psychology — but they are blind to the temperament and ideals of the people to whom they return and who are the work-force, the hands and limbs, of their government. They remain unaware of the immense potential within them, of the spark that made them shake the entire world. Even now we have the same power — the power of faith. Alas, our leaders are either ignorant of Faith or unable to speak the language of faith. True they know the language that can appeal to intellect — though I doubt if these words ever penetrate even that; but the language that can touch the hearts of the people they know not. They cannot speak to their own people in words that may go deep into the heart and evoke the highest degree of commitment and sacrifice — the language of faith, the language of the Qur'ān, the language of the Companions. How can they make their people understand if they cannot speak their language!

What a pity that Muslim leaders speak to their people in the idiom of the West! It is not the idiom of the West, but the uplifting language of faith and the Qur'ān that the people who follow the Prophet, peace be upon him, can understand, which can inspire them to great and greater heights of sacrifice. Speak in their homes and streets, in their mosques and market-places; but let them know you believe what they believe, you cherish what they cherish, you are Muslims as they are. This can happen only if you speak the language of transcendent realities that have been cherished by the people for fourteen hundred years. Therefore I say to you, if you want to touch the hearts of your own people, you must use the language of faith.

I do not oppose modern arts and sciences — I congratulate

you rather, and your guardians who sent you here. Learn as much as you can and do more: undertake original research, add to the store, for it is a great need of our time. But do not confuse means and ends. This walking stick helps me walk — it may even help me defend myself — but it cannot take the place of any objective to which I aspire. If I can get a better stick or if I am able to do without it, I shall then throw it away. So too is human knowledge a means.

And this argument of old and new, modern and ancient, in human knowledge, I have never accepted it. For me knowledge remains ever fresh and new. What you call ancient branches, ancient modes, of learning, were once modern. And what today are proudly presented as modern modes may become old and stale in fifty years — instead of with pride you may think of them, then, with shame. No — the old and new is meaningless quibbling. Learn what there is to learn, languages, arts, sciences, history, philosophy, psychology — but treat these as only a means for achieving your goals.

The disintegrational friction rampant in our countries — which I consider entirely unnecessary and a great wastage of our energies — is mainly because our leaders are inhabitants of the West. Their bodies live in the East, their minds and souls in the West. Yet the people among whom they live, with whom their own destiny is linked can be moved only as Muslims.

You are not the heirs of some barbaric primitive tribe that has suddenly been confronted in its mental and moral darkness with the light of modern technology — you should not then gape open-mouthed at the marvels of electricity and aeroplanes or whatever. You are the heirs of a civilisation that once rescued the world from darkness and destruction, which led mankind. The Arabs, who were the first to embrace Islam, did save humanity when there was none to steer it out of dangerous waters. We have a fundamental difference with the West, we cannot believe blindly in it. It was only because of our own shortcomings and the shortsightedness of our leaders that the Islamic countries have lagged behind in education and learning. The West has overtaken us. Very well. It is no doubt our misfortune, but there is no denying the fact that it was we who showed the world the way to knowledge and progress. Civilisation was committed to our trust, and even today no people except the Islamic people have the capability to conduct humanity to safety. Witness how the West has managed world affairs.

THE WEST'S SHORTCOMINGS

The West has, without doubt, filled the earth with innumerable novel inventions that achieve what it was never thought possible to achieve. Some time back a European scientist proudly told an Indian philosopher that the West had produced aircraft that could cross the wide Atlantic in a few hours, and then narrated other victories of technology. The Indian philosopher listened patiently and when the other had finished, commented: 'You, you have learnt to fly in the sky like the birds (or better) and to swim in the oceans like the fish (or better), but you have still not learnt how to walk on the earth like human beings'. The comment epitomises the achievements of the West — they are still groping in the dark about their ultimate objective.

The first and foremost thing one needs to know and should try to know is the reality of man — what is the ultimate end of human life; what should be done to realise it? The West has not and does not shed light on these questions; that is why its achievements are, finally, a sort of play-acting to avoid those questions. As any dramatic performance is enjoyable, so too the West's exploits on land or sea or in space are enjoyable. But then what? What is the result of so much technological progress?

I ask you, you should ask yourselves, has man become more humane? Have men really come nearer to each other or to nature? Have love and compassion increased or have they decreased? Have men learnt to keep peace with one another? Does the individual find greater peace and contentment of heart? Have men drawn away from cruelty, lewdness, ruthlessness; have they learnt not to take delight in subduing others, robbing, plundering, enslaving, humiliating their fellow human beings? Has it yet dawned on Western man that so far he has been treating the world as (to use Iqbal's phrase) a 'gambler's den' and, in the pursuit of profit or power, taken humanity through the catastrophe of two world wars?

Indeed it is well to ask what has been the result of technological progress, what will be its end? I ask you, what has man gained by it? We see today ever more ill-will, more enmity, among individuals and among the comity of nations. Acts of flagrant injustice are carried out in broad daylight with no better reason than the power to do so. Take the instance of Palestine: the powerful nations of the West banished the inhabitants of that country to make it the national home of another people who had already been settled in other lands for many hundreds of years. All appeals to equity and justice have failed to affect the conscience of the powerful nations of the West. Do you still call their world a civilised world? Has any big power — America or Britain or Russia — the moral courage even to acknowledge the injustice done to the Arabs? How many people are there in this country with the courage to risk admitting that the promises made in their name to the Arabs were broken by their leaders, acting in their name? You will not find another like example of wanton injustice and immorality. But this is only a conspicuous instance of a weird and crazy destructiveness aimed by the West against the whole human race — animated by mutual jealousy and distrust the big nations are arming themselves with weapons capable of destroying the whole of humanity in a few seconds — the rest of the world's nations are the theatre in which this deadly confrontation is being staged.

America and Russia already have such an arsenal; China, Britain and France, are in steady pursuit of the same goal. It is as if some heartless stupid adult had given daggers to little children to play with, knowing that the children were all too willing, all too able, to attack and kill each other — God knows when one of them will try to give the other a death blow.

THE ROLE OF YOUTH
You belong to the Islamic nations and peoples — who have an ideal, a set of beliefs and convictions. Your people will never be content with the materialistic civilisation of the West. By all means, gain what knowledge you can, but as a means, that only: by no means accept the worldview of the

West as the last word, nor as an ultimate end. Nor think of the Western nations as guardians of the world. You are not right, nor have any right, to think of the Eastern nations as uncivilised peoples for whose enlightenment the West must act the part of ministering angel. No. Take from the West that which you need and your people need — do not deny to yourself, nor to them, your and their heritage. The West needs to learn from the East — a life of goodness and virtue is as much an essential for genuine success in this world as in the next; a knowledge of, a capacity to entertain, the idea that human life must serve a higher end, gives to human endeavour (to technology) its proper place and its proper dignity and measure. If you are unable to learn what the West has to teach, it will mean, at worst, a little delay in material progress, some inconvenience and a little more effort for the East to catch up with the West. This explains the difference between the worth of what the West possesses and the way of life chosen by your people in the Islamic East. And now I leave you to decide which of the two is worthier and more valuable.

Chapter Sixteen

Message to Young Muslims in the West

In this written message to those young Muslims who come to the West to undertake higher studies, or who live here, Nadwi exhorts them to make full use of the opportunities that have been placed at their disposal by God.

In the context of the failure of Western civilisation and its tragic consequences, which he has dwelt upon in considerable detail, only in following the path of faith, as illumined by the lives and teachings of the Prophets of God, lies any hope for the future of man. While many ancient faiths have lost their origins, Islam still retains its links with its sources. It possesses the Qur'ān as it was revealed, the authentic record of the sayings and actions of the Prophet, peace be upon him, the vast treasure-house of Sharī'ah and the still vibrant, even though weak, enthusiasm and zeal.

Young Muslims, whether studying or working, have twofold responsibilities: one, to undertake a fresh study of Islam and forge a living contact with the Qur'ān and the life of the Prophet, peace be upon him; and, two, to boldly invite their fellow human beings to Islam, both by their example and their words. Let this unique opportunity not be wasted.

[Ed.]

16

Friends: From across the oceans I send you my best wishes and warmest greetings that reflect my sincere fellowship in Islam. I believe your journey to Europe or America or your sojourn at one of the West's educational or cultural centres was no act of impulse nor chance occurrence, but an act of conscious choice, deliberate decision. It is not a calamity. On the contrary — whether your journey be for a few days or a permanent migration, and whatever its final objectives — it is an opportunity and a favour conferred by God. It is a blessing for you but also for the social environment in which you find yourselves — the modern world, the world of Europe and America and Russia. This is an opportunity that will promote and strengthen your faith in Islam, in the Holy Qur'ān, in the call of the Messengers and in the teachings of the Prophet Muhammad, peace be upon him. In the full glare of the new learning which, after a long period of social and intellectual stagnation, brought about in Europe a revolution in the world of thought and gave to its people a new lease of life, in its full glare you can reflect upon the eternal value of the message of Islam.

THE WESTERN WORLDVIEW

The champions of the modern world will point to its achievements as proof that a civilised society can come into being independently of spiritual convictions, of religious beliefs and moral values, and independently of Prophetic teachings. They will go further and say that this is as it should be; that the foundations of society should rest on knowledge and science, on trade and industry, on political and economic stability, on nationalism and patriotism, on legal and constitutional covenants and orders. Then they will insist that social progress is related exclusively to modern means and machines, the products of their physical sciences. The success

An article written for the Islamic Centre, Geneva, and published in Al-Muslimūn, *Cairo in 1961.*

of their system, the better material conditions of their people, make it certain — they will say — that man should subdue the world, all the forces of nature, to satisfy his material needs, the appetites of the body. Man's salvation lies in science and technology. Past failure was due simply to the fact that the channels for the exchange and implementation of ideas were blocked, that the world was divided into different, insufficiently linked parts.

The West has for a long time propagated this view and done so with fanatical enthusiasm. Its slogans are — there is no god, no religion, no unseen, no spirit, no Hereafter. According to the West, the *Sharī'ah* and its social-spiritual structure are mere superstition. The real elements of life are perception, experience, profit, nationalism, democracy, communism. The champions of this worldview have many schools of thought; they all left their imprints on thought and society. But the common denominator to all of them is materialism.

Now the West is in a position openly to enforce its viewpoint — a unique event in world history made possible by the phenomenal resources, military and economic, the West can dispose for the imposition of its culture on the rest of the world. An unparalleled achievement — even the most culturally and intellectually gifted peoples of past history could not establish such total and universal ascendancy. When Europe embarked on its course of material progress and expansion there was no power to challenge or impede it. The Church had long since capitulated to the intellectual-political revolt within Christianity. The Islamic East yielded to its intellectual and political might in the nineteenth century, and the world has gone on submitting, quietly and quickly.

THE TRAGIC CONSEQUENCES
Europe captured the world stage; yet the drama of materialism, conceived and acted by brilliant human intellects is coming to its tragic end; the system of the West has proved a colossal failure. Discord and confusion, internal and external, are everywhere apparent: individuals, classes, communities, nations are in desperate competition with each

other, and the immediate horizon is dark with the threat of major war, a disaster that would end humanity altogether. Self-contentment, peace, serenity are things of the past. Man is haunted by fear. His soul is restless, anxious; the moral and spiritual void deepens; amid distress, misery, frustration, there is a feeling of bitter despondency everywhere because the mess seems quite irrecoverable, quite beyond remedy.

The wretchedness and infelicity of Western civilisation needs to be pointed out again and again — for, in the East, there are still people who believe in its progressiveness and success, who look upon it with envy and respect, even religious reverence. You who now live in the midst of this civilisation can see at first hand the anxious unease of the people, and evidence everywhere of decay and degeneration. You will observe its typical characteristics in the moral attitude of its political leaders, in the general disregard for human sentiments, in the neglect of ethical values, in the high incidence of crime, of all kinds of moral offences. You will see it most clearly in the obdurate refusal of the West's leaders, political or intellectual, to even appreciate the essence of humanity, let alone to heed the call of the spirit and guide the human community to its high destiny, to achieve harmony and integration. The civilisation of the West, at the height of its organisation and culture, is now living its crisis of confidence.

This state of affairs should make it evident to you that a society not based on Faith is doomed to an evil fate, it may manage to prolong its life a little more — it is bound to come to a tragic end. Surely no-one really believes that this civilisation cannot perish, that it cannot become insolvent.

Truly, the path of Faith is the path of the Prophets of God; it lies in their teachings and lives. It is their message which uplifts the character of individuals and communities alike, that irradiates and strengthens them from within. The examples of the Prophets impart faith and courage independently of academics or educational institutions or any means of mass propaganda, mass communication. Sincere faith transmutes greed, hypocrisy, vaunting ostentation, the love of power; it generates confidence in the Hereafter and, by convincing man of the transitoriness of worldly joys and

188

sorrows, encourages him to use his resources in the service of God. For, it is in that service of God that man attains his true dignity. Repeatedly in human history, men of faith have rescued society from the depths of degeneracy; in earnest solicitude for the deliverance of mankind preserved it from destruction and taught the higher human values. History will always remember them.

It is true that the ancient faiths, which in the past served mankind and whose contribution to the lifting up of human society is unforgettable, have since lost their vitality and force. Even those who nominally believed in these religions have lost faith in them — they are not equipped to meet the demands of the present times and have, all but completely, capitulated to Western civilisation as though in agreement that materialism is the last stage in the evolution of human society.

THE ROLE OF ISLAM

But at this critical juncture one religion persists — it lives in its original form, and its followers know that they must see that it continues so, for they have been entrusted with the superintendence of the world, the survival of civilisation, the close examination of the good and evil propensities of mankind. They know that they will be held to account for the way they discharge their duty. Islam is distinguished above other faiths in four crucial respects:

First, it possesses the Qur'ān, whose abundant and inexhaustible wisdom is an everlasting source of joy and encouragement to man to use all his powers of body, heart and soul, and reason, in the way of God and for the benefit of all mankind. This book brought about a mighty revolution in the lives of millions of men and women — unchanged and unaltered for fourteen hundred years, it can do so again.

Secondly, Islam possesses the vast, fragrant treasures of the sayings and actions of its Blessed Prophet, Muhammad, bright and beautiful. This record is the most radiant in the life of mankind; it reminds man of his true position; it revives in him his sense of dignity. Its beauty is such that it cannot but inspire all men to follow it and attain heights of power and purity and peace. It unravels the knots that entangle human intellect; it brings out hidden realities. It remains intact, though ages have passed.

Thirdly, the treasure of the Islamic *Sharī'ah* is preserved intact and unadulterated, as it was left by the Prophet himself, peace be upon him. The *Sharī'ah* is the most perfect jurisprudential system in the world. It combines admirably the ancient and the modern and itself enables the construction, upon its wise and sound foundations, of a healthy social system in every age and clime.

Fourthly, the adherents of Islam are characterised by an enthusiasm for their faith such as no other community can show. In spite of their apparent lethargy the Muslim people will rise in readiness for their faith and be capable of the highest sacrifice in the way of Allah — if an earnest leader calls them. This is a resource of which the Western nations are devoid.

TO THE MUSLIM YOUTH

Let me now remind you, young Muslim men and women, residents or students in Europe and America, that you are Muslims and a part of the great Islamic *Millah*. You are members of one international family, heirs to the one great legacy. By 'family' I do not mean blood ties; nor do I mean by 'legacy' what in their ignorance or malice the scholars or Orientalists intend when they write on 'The Legacy of Islam'. I mean that brotherhood of the deeply committed servants of God, who may have earned a place of distinction by doing their level best in the path of faith and learning by dint of their services and sacrifice and struggle.

You should undertake a fresh study of Islam in the light of what I have said so far. Try to understand it in a new way, along new lines, seriously and sincerely. You should study the Qur'ān not with the aid of commentaries but with the depth of your hearts and minds. Use your perspicacity and your judgement while learning it. You should read it as if it were not an old scripture but one sent down for the present age, or, rather, one that is being revealed to you directly. Spend your precious time on the study of the life of the Prophet, peace be upon him, and his Traditions; try to forge a living contact with him. This contact you should base on love, on devoted, dedicated study, on respect and on the will to obey.

Next, do your duty as the true representatives of Islam in the West. Assert boldly the tenets of your faith, present a correct image of it, and safeguard its teachings, commands and practices. You are representatives of the best of religions, the one ideally suited to modern times. You need your faith as it needs you. Set a good example to those young men — coming from Muslim countries or receiving education at Arab institutions — who may be shy of being known as Muslims. Appeal to your friends, teachers and neighbours by leading a truly Islamic life of piety and truthfulness, Prayer and remembrance of God, dignified contentment and manly joy. History tells that Islam has drawn to itself countless intellectuals in this way and conquered whole nations and communities without shedding a drop of blood.

You may be on the register of a university, or work in a factory or an office. Whatever your station, your life is, by virtue of your faith and its message, most exalted. Islam attaches the greatest importance to rendering to everyone his due. You owe certain duties to your teachers from whom you may have learnt something; fulfil your responsibility with regard to them, be their guide and mentor, so that they understand Islam properly.

I say to you again, your stay in Europe or America is a unique opportunity, God-given, from which you should derive the fullest advantage. Through it you can also pave the way for the resurgence of Islam and the well-being of mankind. Your presence in these lands will be a source of strength to your faith; it will lead to trust and reliance on it, and new avenues for the progress of Islam will open as a result.

You are at a place where the blessing of Islam has been non-existent for a long time. The way of life there is inimical to the Divine message and the levels of Prophetic teachings; it is inimical to moral and spiritual values. Your presence can help alleviate this dreadful condition of void if you do not become its slaves but choose instead to be true Muslims, the slaves of God.